Closers, Openers, Revisiters, Energizers

Activities and Games for Technical Training

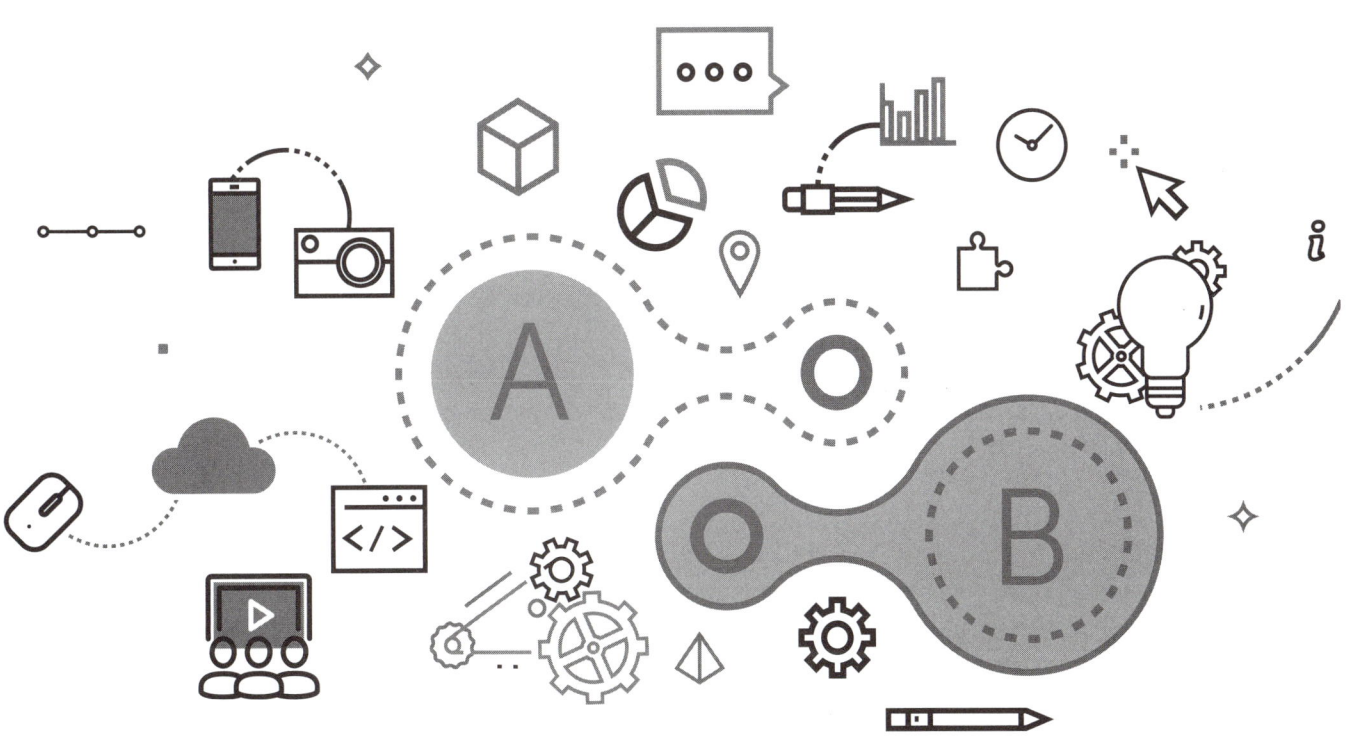

Vol. 4

By The Bob Pike Group

☐ ☐ ☐ CORE: ACTIVITIES AND GAMES FOR TECHNICAL TRAINING, CLOSERS, OPENERS, REVISITERS, ENERGIZERS, VOL. 4

by
Becky Pike Pluth, M.ED., CSP
Rich Meiss, MBA
Karen Carlson
Scott Enebo, M.A.
Janice Horne
Marc Ratcliffe, M.ED.
Adrianne Roggenbuck, M.ED.
Priscilla Shumway, M.ED.

Cover Design by Imagewerks
Internal Layout by Alan Pranke
Compiled and Edited by Rich Meiss
Copy Editing and Proofreading by Liz Wheeler

©2017 Creative Training Productions, LLC
Text copyright: Becky Pike Pluth, Rich Meiss, Karen Carlson, Scott Enebo, Janice Horne, Marc Ratcliffe, Adrianne Roggenbuck and Priscilla Shumway.

ALL RIGHTS RESERVED

Permission is granted by the authors for the purchaser of this book to copy and use designated pages only in seminars and meetings. Unless specifically designated, no part of this publication may be reproduced, stored in a retrieval system, or transmitted in any form or by any means, electronic, mechanical, photocopy, scanning or otherwise except as permitted under the United States 1976 Copyright Act or by written permission from the publisher.

ISBN: 978-0-9896615-5-3

10 9 8 7 6 5 4 3 2

Printed in the United States of America

Publisher
Creative Training Productions LLC
14530 Martin Drive
Eden Prairie MN 55344

For additional books or quantity discounts, contact:
The Bob Pike Group
Phone: 800-383-9210 and 952-829-1954
Fax: 952-829-0260
Email: info@bobpikegroup.com

THANK YOU TO MENTORS, COLLEAGUES AND CLIENTS

We thank our many mentors, colleagues and clients with whom we've had the privilege of working throughout our careers in the training and human resource development field. You have sharpened our minds and helped us develop many of the concepts which we now teach.

Thank you to the tens of thousands of presenters, trainers and facilitators with whom we've worked over the last 30+ years. Many of you have given us great ideas, and/or allowed us to try out these ideas in your sessions. We appreciate the chance to work with so many great people, and would also welcome any feedback on the exercises in this book.*

We extend a special thank you to the training consultants of The Bob Pike Group. Karen, Scott, Janice, Marc, Bob, Adrianne, and Priscilla — you bring a professionalism and passion to your training that makes it a joy to work together. Thank you for your commitment to participant-centered training and for your creativity in putting together these exercises.

Thank you to Imagewerks, Alan Pranke and Liz Wheeler for your graphic design and editing skills.

And a special thanks to the loves of our lives, Brad Pluth and Barbara Meiss, for your encouragement and continued support of projects like these.

Becky Pike Pluth and Rich Meiss

I'd like to extend a very special thank you to Rich Meiss for creating the CORE brand with our dear friend Doug McCallum and for his tireless work on this project.

Becky Pike Pluth

*See *"Your Name in Lights"* on page 121 for a way to contribute your own activity to another version of this book.

CONTENTS

Introduction 7
How to Use this Book 9
Closers 11
    Breaker Box 12
    Capture and Share the Knowledge 15
    Change Exchange 17
    Clue 19
    Elevator Pitch 21
    How Much is it Worth? 23
    Koosh Toss Revisit 25
    Phone Reminder 27
    Road Signs 28
    Showdown 31
    TA-DA Closer 32
    Visual Summary 35
Openers 37
    Computer Classroom Set-Up 38
    Curtains Up, Curtains Down 41
    Experience Line-Up 43
    Garage Window 44
    Get Puzzled 47
    If You Can Do That 48
    Letter Scramble 51
    Map It! 53
    Nuts and Bolts 55
    Origins of Expressions 56
    Seek and Find 59
    Think Outside the Training Room Box 61
    True/False Anticipation Guide 62

Revisiters 65
- Buyers and Sellers 67
- Class Replay 68
- Command Keeper Revisit 71
- Computer Application Window Pane 73
- Computer Quiz Carousel 75
- Create Your Own Job Aid 77
- Focus Group 79
- "Label This" Relay 80
- Magnet Word Summary 82
- Name that Part 85
- Race to the Finish 87
- Technical Term Trip Up 89
- What's Wrong with this Picture? 91
- Which Comes First? 93

Energizers 95
- Can You Top This? 97
- Face to Face 99
- I Fought the Law 100
- I Heard That! 102
- Keyboard Kinesthetics 105
- Learning Passport 106
- Process Steps Pop Up 109
- Reorganization 111
- Technical Anagrams 113
- Training Musical Chairs 115
- Virtual Tour 117
- Zip Zap Zop 119

Your Name in Lights 121
About the Authors 123

INTRODUCTION

Much so-called technical training today is a dull combination of show and tell. Because most technical trainers and presenters are given little time to creatively prepare their sessions, they use the easiest and most common form of delivery – lecture. Yet we know from research that if participants are exposed to an idea only one time, they will remember less than 10 percent after 24 hours. Just because you said it doesn't mean they learned it!

If we can involve the learners through group discussions and activities, we increase the retention rate to as high as 50 percent. And if we can have participants applying and even teaching the content to each other, retention soars as high as 90 percent.

These user-friendly activities and practical exercises are some of the best The Bob Pike Group trainers have used in Creative Training Techniques and our other seminars for more than 30 years. They work! Spice up your technical training with applicable openers and closers. Revisit your content in new and fresh ways. Stimulate and engage your participants with fast energizers. The great news is you don't have to spend time coming up with these exercises – they are right here at your fingertips!

This CORE book is organized to help you quickly determine which activity or exercise will work for you and your audience. Choose from these four categories:

Closers – to help tie things together and end a session with impact,

Openers – to begin a session in a powerful way and draw participants into the content,

Revisiters – to reinforce key learning in fresh and engaging ways, and

Energizers – to keep participants mentally stimulated and physically activated throughout.

This is a cookbook. Rather than reading every page and trying every recipe, use the table of contents to choose what you're hungriest for right now. We know that as you do, you'll provide a great learning "meal" for your participants – and along the way, you'll enjoy the process greatly. All good wishes!

Rich Meiss
MBA, MPCT, Senior Training Consultant for The Bob Pike Group

HOW TO USE THIS BOOK

Here are four simple steps for using this book effectively:

1. Remind yourself why it is important to use closers, openers, revisiters and energizers by reading the first page of each chapter.

2. Select the appropriate category – closers, openers, revisiters or energizers.

3. Pick the best exercise for your content and purpose.

4. Practice, practice and practice the exercise before you actually use it.

Why use Closers, Openers, Revisiters and Energizers?

Each chapter gives more detail about the reasons to use these CORE exercises in your presentations, but here is a general overview.

Too many presentations simply start and end without a process or purpose. Yet research reveals that people remember best what they see or hear first and last, so we need to start strong and end strong – using good openers and closers. The purpose of revisiters is to make sure the participants really learn the content. A favorite phrase we use is "just because you said it doesn't mean they learned it." Review multiple times with a variety of methods to ensure learning takes place. And energizers are used to keep participants awake and attentive in the session.

What categories are included in this book?

Although many of these exercises can be used for multiple purposes, we have divided them into four key categories, with energizers having two subcategories:

Closers

Openers

Revisiters

Energizers

They are the CORE to help you CORE and win in your presentations. Each exercise has been placed into one of these categories and put in that section of the book. In addition, we have often indicated that the exercise may be used for another purpose. For example, several of the revisiter techniques are also good energizers.

Closers, Openers, Revisiters, Energizers

CLOSERS

The most important training "real estate" is the beginning and ending of your session because this information is what gets remembered the most easily! It's the rule of primacy and recency. So when you're training, don't use your closing as a way to promote the evaluation form, or worse yet, just end! Close your session with impact and purpose. Make sure that you have a closing ACT.

A closing ACT includes **A**ction planning, **C**elebration, and **T**ying things together.

Action planning gives participants time to reflect on the important concepts or ideas learned in the session and create a plan on how they will use the information back on the job. Multiple studies have shown that when people commit to making changes, they are much more likely to follow through. And when people plan the logistics of how and when they will make those changes, the probability increases even more. Use your closing time to help them achieve this!

Celebration gives participants who have invested time, energy and perhaps even money a chance to relish the new insights and skills they have gained as a result of the training. During your time together, they've made difficult decisions, solved tough problems, or provided valuable input. All of these are reasons to celebrate their investment and revel in these accomplishments!

Celebration can take many forms. It might be something formal, such as certificates of completion given out at a training event, or it might be informal celebration with the awarding of small prizes, congratulations from the boss, or even just a quick high-five among the group members.

Tie things together when you close. A great presentation comes full circle. Training sessions circle back to the stated objectives to make sure participants are satisfied with the outcomes. An opening exercise that is used is referred to again as the program is concluded. Then close with a powerful ending – a quote, story, question, or call to action.

Here are some great, proven technical training closers for you to use.

http://bit.ly/CORETTClosers

Closers, Openers, Revisiters, Energizers

BREAKER BOX

Author: Scott Enebo

Description: Learners will use a graphic of a breaker box to revisit key content from the training.

Objective: To let learners check in to see what information they have mastered and where they still need some more exposure or work

Time: 3-5 minutes

Audience: Any training audience

Group Size: Any

Materials:
- Paper and pen
- Image of breaker box with content ideas listed

Process:
1. Create a simple breaker box like the image to the right and write your key content areas beside each of the breakers.

2. Give learners a copy of that breaker box handout.

3. Say, "Working on your own, look at the content topics listed on your breaker box. By the end of our session, we want to ensure that all of these are in the 'ON' position so that we can be as effective as possible back on the job. While we still have more information to cover, I would like to see where each of us is at and where we might still be 'OFF' so that we can answer questions that still need addressing. As you look at each item, circle ON if you are all set, or OFF if you are still in need of more information or clarification."

4. Allow time for learners to work quietly on their own.

5. Say, "Please turn to a partner and share what you marked. If there is something that your partner has marked as OFF and it is content that we have covered, see if you are able to help fill in the gaps. If you cannot provide the information, be sure to bring those questions to the group's attention so that we can address them."

6. Address questions as needed after sharing.

Debrief: This activity does not require a formal debrief as the partner sharing fulfills this. After everyone has shared, here are some questions that you may choose to ask:

- What were some areas that you found you were both stuck on?
- What was something that your partner helped you better understand so that you were able to flip your breaker to ON?
- What do you still have in the OFF position that you are looking forward to covering today?

Variations:
- This is an excellent opportunity to use an Audience Response System ("clickers") to let learners weigh in on the items instead of doing it on paper. This makes responses anonymous, so you are more likely to get honest responses that will help you find the gaps where people are still unclear.
- Instead of having a standard agenda, create it in the image of a breaker box. As you cover content, you can indicate in some fashion that the switch is thrown from "OFF" to "ON" as you show progress in the class.

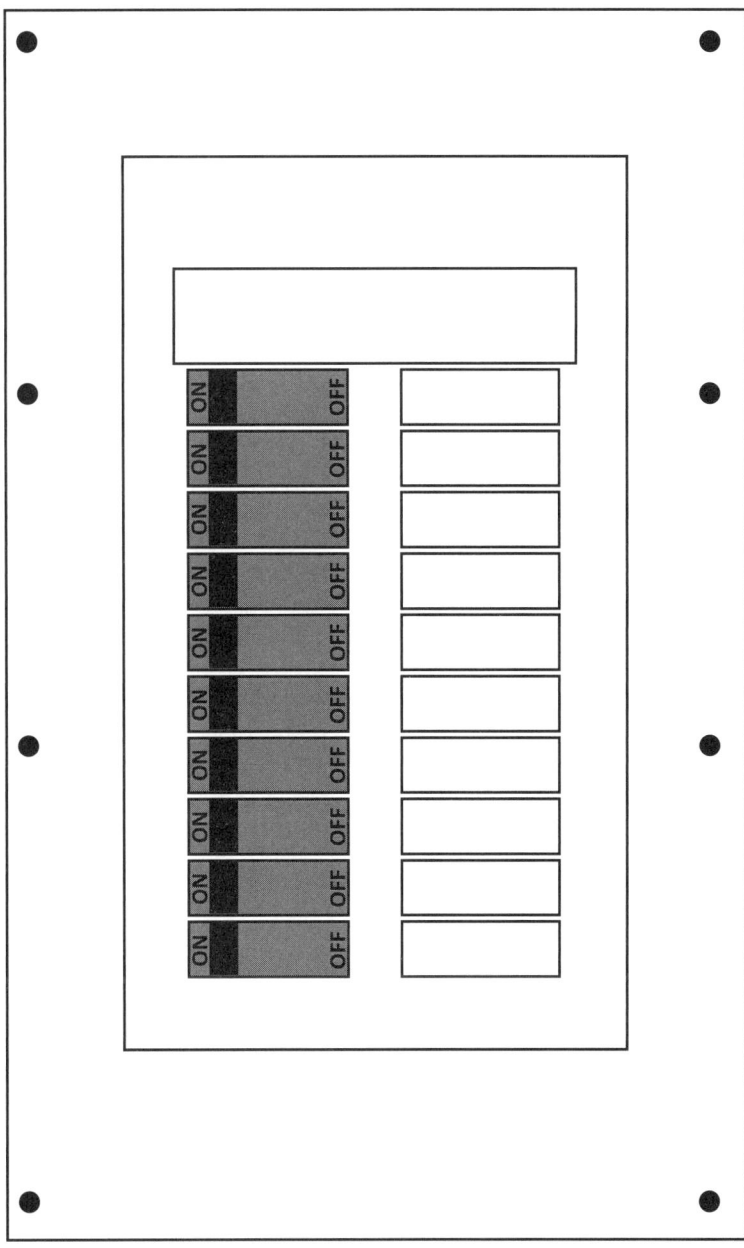

Closers, Openers, Revisiters, Energizers

CAPTURE AND SHARE THE KNOWLEDGE ☐ ☐ ☐

Author: Karen Carlson

Description: Have participants take pictures of workshop visuals such as flip charts at the end of the training.

Objective: To utilize electronic gadgets (smart phones, tablets, laptops, etc.) to photograph or document content used or created in class to encourage transfer of training from the classroom to the job

Time: 5 minutes

Audience: Any technical training audience where technology is commonplace

Group Size: Any size

Materials: Electronic gadgets brought to class by participants

Process: As class is about to close, have participants wander around the classroom to capture (photograph) flip charts and other content they want to be sure to remember and share back on the job. Each participant then attaches his or her photographs to a meeting invite in 30/60/90 days as a way to check in with himself or herself regarding how much content each participant has retained and applied.

Debrief: None, or a quick debrief by simply asking participants to share examples of content they will revisit and share back on the job.

Variations: Participants may opt to attach the photographs and notes to a meeting invite for their team so they can share what they learned with those who were unable to attend the training session.

Closers, Openers, Revisiters, Energizers

CHANGE EXCHANGE

Author: Becky Pike Pluth

Description: Participants team up to share valuable learning points and are rewarded with coins; the value of the coin given is dependent upon how valuable the learning point is to the recipient.

Objective: To help participants determine what the best takeaways or learnings are from the session

Time: 10 minutes

Audience: Any technical training audience. If outside the United States, modify the currency. Groups that are not opposed to sharing their opinion and determining good ideas from great ideas.

Group Size: 8 or more participants

Materials:
- One 4"x6" card per person
- Small denominations of coin based on the currency of your location. The majority of the change should be pennies and nickels or the equivalent. Make sure to have at least one quarter per table.
- Chime (optional)

Process:
1. Have participants take 60 seconds and write down their best takeaways/learnings from the course on a 4"x6" card.
2. Then have them select change from either their change purse or from what you have put on the table. Each person should have a variety, like two pennies and two nickels, perhaps a dime and a few people should have a quarter.
3. Have them go around the room finding one partner at a time. If you're in a computer-based classroom, have learners stand and share with someone in the row behind and the row ahead or beside.
4. With the partner, have them share a learning takeaway and hear a learning takeaway. Once both partners have shared, they exchange a coin with one another based on how creative or helpful the takeaway idea was. (A penny would be "helpful or creative," a nickel would be "really helpful or creative," a dime or quarter would be "extremely helpful or creative.")
5. Ring the chime to remind participants to rotate to a new person.

Debrief: At the end of a couple minutes, those who received a quarter will share with the group their most helpful or creative action ideas.

Variations: If it is a group with fewer than six people, have them share their "quarter" thought with the entire group.

http://bit.ly/CORETTChangeEx

Closers, Openers, Revisiters, Energizers

17

http://bit.ly/CORETTClue

CLUE

Author: Becky Pike Pluth

Description: One participant attempts to use words to describe a concept covered during class to get a team to correctly name the concept.

Objective: To help participants recall and revisit different key terms, content areas or pieces of technical information

Time: 10 minutes

Audience: Any technical training audience with a common language

Group Size: 10 or more participants

Materials:
- 5-10 PowerPoint slides. Each slide should have one concept or idea from the content covered. Black screens are added in-between each concept slide.
- Dice: One die per group
- Candy/Prize (optional)

Process:
1. Separate the participants in the room into groups of 3-5 people. In a computer classroom, this is easily done by row.
2. Explain to the group that a volunteer will be attempting to get the remainder of the group to guess a word, phrase, or concept from the technical training class in a 15-30 second window.
3. After 15-30 seconds pass, the slide automatically advances to a black screen.
4. Teams that guessed the concept before it moved to the black screen roll their die and score the number of points they roll.
5. Rotate the volunteer position to a new team member and repeat the steps.
6. Repeat the steps as many times as time allows or for as much revisiting as the group needs.
7. Optional: The group with the largest number of points at the end wins a candy/small prize.

Debrief: None

Variations:
- If the group is competitive or good natured, have all teams roll at the end of each time slot. Those groups that did not get the answer in time receive negative points.
- This exercise can also be used to teach new content to the group. Show one slide, do the activity, roll the die for teams that guessed accurately and then lecture on the point. Then show another slide and repeat the process. This can make a section of "dry, boring, technical content" come to life in what I call an "Interactive Lecturette." The lectures should only last 4-8 minutes.

Closers, Openers, Revisiters, Energizers

ELEVATOR PITCH ☐ ☐ ☐

Author: Priscilla Shumway

Description: Participants prepare an elevator speech describing the training content to their bosses.

Objective: To help participants focus on key learning points and articulate the benefits

Time: 5-10 minutes

Audience: Any technical training audience

Group Size: Any size, but usually a smaller group of 20 or fewer

Materials:
- Paper
- Pencil

Process:
1. Tell the participants to imagine that they have just met their boss in the elevator at work. The boss asks them what the training class was all about and how it will help the participant when he or she returns to work.

2. Give each participant two minutes to write down the 15-second elevator pitch.

3. Depending on the size of the group, have the participants share these at their tables. Each team then chooses one elevator pitch to be presented to the large group.

Debrief: None

Variations: If it is a small group of fewer than six people, have each of them share their pitches with the entire group.

Closers, Openers, Revisiters, Energizers

HOW MUCH IS IT WORTH? ☐ ☐ ☐

Author: Karen Carlson

Description: Participants guess the numeric answer to a question without going over the right number.

Objective: To consider the impact (cost, time, etc.) if behavior change does or does not occur

Time: 5 minutes

Audience: Any training audience

Group Size: Any, although it is easiest to manage with groups of 12 or fewer people

Materials:
- Large index cards or regular sheets of paper and markers or white boards and dry-erase markers
- Pre-conceived questions based on the content that require an answer that has a number

Process:
1. Have participants sit or stand in a row facing you, the trainer. Pose questions to the group that require numeric answers. Questions should involve implications (decreased costs, time lost, productivity increases, etc.) based on whether the changes covered in the training take place or not. Sample questions would be: How much does each production error cost? How much will productivity increase by using the new machine or process?

2. Have participants write their answers on their cards. The person with the answer closest to the correct answer without going over gets a point.

3. Have participants either use a new card or clean the white board for each new question. The first participant to five points wins. Prizes are optional.

Debrief: Emphasize the fact that each participant plays a key role in the results of this change.

Variations: You may choose to add questions that do not require numeric answers, such as who is responsible for a given task, what are the consequences for not doing the given task, etc. You can give points based on how accurate the answers are.

Closers, Openers, Revisiters, Energizers

KOOSH TOSS REVISIT

Author: Janice Horne

Description: Participants toss a Koosh ball onto a grid with training topics to see which topic they will review.

Objective: Participants revisit training content in a fun and active way

Time: 10 minutes

Audience: Any technical training audience

Group Size: 16 or fewer

Materials:
- Flip chart paper with four quadrants drawn on it; each quadrant should be labeled with a main topic from the training.
- Koosh (porcupine) ball. The soft kind works best.

Process:
1. Invite participants to join you at an open space in the room.
2. Place the paper on the floor.
3. Have participants form teams of 3-5 people. The members of the team will stand behind each other facing the paper on the floor. Designate a line approximately three feet (one meter) back from the bottom edge of the paper.
2. Inform participants that they will each have an opportunity to throw the Koosh ball onto the paper. They will then say one thing they learned about the topic on which the ball lands. Then they go to the back of their team line.
3. Rotate from one group to the next until each participant has had a chance to throw the ball and share a key learning.

Debrief: None

Variations:
- Give participants two minutes to review information they have learned around the four topics you placed on the paper, either alone or as a group. Then tear the poster off and invite participants to an open space in the room for the activity.
- Allow participants to confer with team members before answering.

Closers, Openers, Revisiters, Energizers

PHONE REMINDER ☐ ☐ ☐

Author: Janice Horne

Description: Participants pair and share action plans by placing a reminder on their phones or tablets.

Objective: To provide for action-planning and accountability

Time: 5 minutes

Audience: Any technical training audience

Group Size: Any size

Materials: 3"x5" card or phone/tablet

Process:
1. Invite participants to take their phones or tablets and go to the reminder section and write one or two actions they plan to take as a result of the training. [For those who do not have a phone or a tablet, invite them to write their actions on a 3"x5" card with their name and e-mail address.]

2. Ask participants to stand up with their phone/tablet or 3"x5" card in hand and find someone in the room with whom to partner. (This may be a learning partner from earlier pairings.) If there is an odd number, there may be one group of three.

3. After everyone is paired up, partners will share the information they had written in the reminder application on their phone/tablet (or 3"x5" card) and also share their contact information. Each partner will then place a reminder on his or her phone to contact his or her partner in two weeks by email or text to see how each is doing on the action plans.

Debrief: None

Variations: Invite participants to open up their Reminder Application and then swap phones with their partners to enter the contact information and action items.

Closers, Openers, Revisiters, Energizers

ROAD SIGNS

Author: Scott Enebo

Description: Use common road signs to help learners reflect on the learning and action plan.

Objective: To close a training session with a structure that helps learners take action on what they have learned

Time: 5-10 minutes

Audience: Any technical training audience

Group Size: Any

Materials:
- One piece of paper or index card per person
- Flip chart paper or PowerPoint slide with road sign graphics

Process:
1. Say, "In just a moment I am going to ask you to think about what you have learned in this class. On your piece of paper, write your answers to each of these questions."

2. Show images of the Yield, Stop and One Way signs on either a chart pad or PowerPoint slide.

3. Say, "Based on what we have covered in this class …

   A. [YIELD sign] …what is something that made you *yield* or pause as you took a closer look at the information?

   B. [STOP sign] … what is something that you are going to *stop* doing because you realize that it is not helping you get the best results?

   C. [ONE WAY sign] … what is *one way* that you are going to implement this information back on the job?"

4. Give participants time to write.

5. Say, "Take a look at what you just wrote. I would like for you to select one of these three items to share with the class. Each person will share one item as we close our session today." If time allows, you can have each learner share all three items on each paper.

6. Give everyone time to share.

Debrief: This closer does not require a debrief as the act of sharing takeaways and action items is the real power in the activity. It helps encourage learners to go and implement new learning back on the job.

Variations:
- You can choose to use this as a carry-over activity where each learner puts his answer on a piece of paper and then places it in an envelope with his mailing address on it. You then can send these out in 30/60/90 days as a reminder to the participants of what they had intended to do following the session to either confirm their actions or else give a chance to make a new effort.

- Use different signs as a way to draw out learning. Consider using ones that are currently being used in the work area so that the sign itself is a reminder of what they wanted to start or stop doing. Some other ideas might be:

    A. — "For our daily work, what is something that you consider a 'Do Not Enter?'"

    B. — "What is a caution that you would give others as they think about implementing this content?"

Closers, Openers, Revisiters, Energizers

SHOWDOWN ☐ ☐ ☐

Author: Marc Ratcliffe

Description: A brief competition that has learners competing to recall workshop content

Objective: Have learners recall session content in a creative way that encourages collaboration as a way of promoting content reinforcement.

Time: 25 minutes

Audience: Any technical training audience

Group Size: 20 or fewer

Materials:
- Flip chart paper
- Pens

Process:
1. Set up the activity by writing six key topics or topic statements from the session on the board or screen.

2. Next, divide the class into two smaller groups.

3. Begin the game by inviting one of the groups to select one of the listed topics. This group then nominates how many answers to that topic they think they can name. For example, in a business leadership class, one of the topics could be "Leadership Theorists" and the group may nominate "six."

4. The group receives points for every correct answer they provide.

5. Once completed, the other group can earn points from the same topic by nominating additional correct answers. They would then select a new topic from the board. This process continues until there are no remaining topics on the board. You, the trainer, tally the points and award a winner.

Debrief: Recognize the participants' participation and raise any additional points as necessary.

Variations: As an extension, Showdown could be used as a self-evaluation tool where participants are asked to internalize the questions and come up with an appropriate amount of responses for each one. For example, statements could include "Things I will immediately apply," "Ideas I will challenge," or "Topics I will research."

Closers, Openers, Revisiters, Energizers

TA-DA CLOSER

Author: Adrianne Roggenbuck

Description: Learners will answer questions on a worksheet to help structure their action planning while also celebrating their learning partners.

Objective: To thank the participants for their participation and create an action plan for implementation of the training

Time: 10 minutes

Audience: Technical group in a computer lab

Group Size: Any size group divided into learning partnerships

Materials:
- Computer with Internet access per participant
- TA-DA template

Process:
1. Provide the participants with the TA-DA template to fill in on their computers.
2. When they have completed the template, have them email it to their learning partner. The learning partner will reply to the email after the training has ended, but within 30 days, to find out how well his or her partner is doing in following the action plan. He or she will also answer the question the partner posed.

Debrief: At the end of the activity, have the group stand and say, "TA-DA!" Then tell them they are ta-done!

Variations: If students do not have Internet access, this activity could be done using index cards that the partners would exchange with each other. They would include their email address on the card in order to send a follow-up email within 30 days.

TA-DA Template

T	**Thank** your partner for helping support your learning in this session. Be specific about how he or she did this.
A	List your top 3-5 **Action** ideas from the session.
D	**Determine** the first step you will take to implement your Action ideas. Prioritize the others.
A	**Ask** your partner a question about a key concept from the session.

Closers, Openers, Revisiters, Energizers

VISUAL SUMMARY ☐ ☐ ☐

Author: Priscilla Shumway

Description: Teams of learners create posters representing training content then try to interpret the other teams' posters.

Objective: To help participants visualize technical information

Time: 15 minutes

Audience: Any training audience learning difficult or complex technical content

Group Size: Any size, but best if fewer than 30 people

Materials:
- Flip chart paper
- Markers

Process:
1. Divide the group into teams of 3-4 people. Each team has a piece of flip chart paper taped to the wall and several colored markers.

2. Tell them to draw a poster that summarizes the key learning points or the steps in one of the processes they learned using only pictures and no text. Depending on the complexity of the process, give them 3-4 minutes to draw.

3. After time is up, have the teams move from poster to poster while trying to guess what the other posters represent.

4. Allow each team to describe its poster and then ask the other teams how they interpreted the posters.

Debrief: Ask questions such as: What posters were easy to decipher? Why? How did the complexity of the topic affect your ability to use pictures to summarize it? Which graphics helped you to guess the point of the poster?

Variations: Have teams guess what the poster represents first and then have the drawing team explain what their poster represents.

Closers, Openers, Revisiters, Energizers

Openers

People remember what they hear first and last the best. So start your training sessions with a bang and not a lot of housekeeping details!

An opener is an activity that gets people thinking about the content and meeting other learners. We use the acronym BAR to help you easily remember the intent of a good opener. Does it **B**reak preoccupation? Does it **A**llow networking? Does it **R**elate to content?

Break preoccupation. Participants come to meetings, presentations and learning events with all kinds of distractions, such as business phone calls to be made, deadlines to be met, or the fight with the kids that morning over unfinished homework. For this reason, a good presenter recognizes that he must break through this preoccupation barrier, because it can be the biggest enemy to capturing the full attention of the participants. The key to breaking preoccupation is involvement. Participants can ignore the presenter, but it is difficult to ignore peers when there is a task to accomplish.

Allow networking. Adults usually come to learning events with some experience in the topic. The good presenter will want to tap into that experience throughout the presentation. To accommodate this, she will get the participants acquainted and comfortable with each other. Then, throughout the session, she will have them share ideas and experiences with each other, thus enhancing the learning for all. Most adults don't want to attend a "sit and get" event; they want to take part, think, contribute and learn.

Networking also reduces tension. Participants come into a learning environment wondering, "Can I contribute? Will I fit in? Will anything make me look or feel foolish?" The faster they get comfortable with each other, the faster they will be open to learning.

Relate to the topic. Most of your participants want practical take-away value. To demonstrate this value right from the start, the strong presenter will begin with an opener that relates to the content. Poor presenters often start with a story or a joke that might be funny but has nothing to do with the content or the event. Make sure your opener has a connection to the topic at hand.

Break preoccupation, Allow networking, and Relate to the content. By following these three suggestions, you will find that your opening will raise the **BAR** of your presentation, meeting or training event. Following are some time-tested technical training openers that meet these criteria.

http://bit.ly/CORETTOpen

COMPUTER CLASSROOM SET-UP

Author: Rich Meiss

Description: Consider alternatives to the typical classroom set-up for training at computers for enhanced learning and engagement.

Objective: To choose an effective classroom set-up to teach more effectively and interactively

Time: No extra class time required once the room is configured according to the diagram

Audience: Any technical training audience learning at computers

Group Size: Usually 16 or fewer people

Materials:
- Computers and chairs
- One of each of the following at each station: nametag, pen and highlighter, sticky notes, a Koosh ball, a large bandana and tape

Process: The ideal room set-up for good computer training is shown here. Notice the following features of this room set-up:

1. The trainer's master system is set in the front of the room, controlled from the front left.

2. Participant computers are set around the outside of the room with the monitors nearly up against the outer walls.

3. Participants are seated at the computers, each paired with another participant who is either more or less experienced at either computer usage in general or in the use of the software being trained. (See the Experience Line Up activity in this book.)

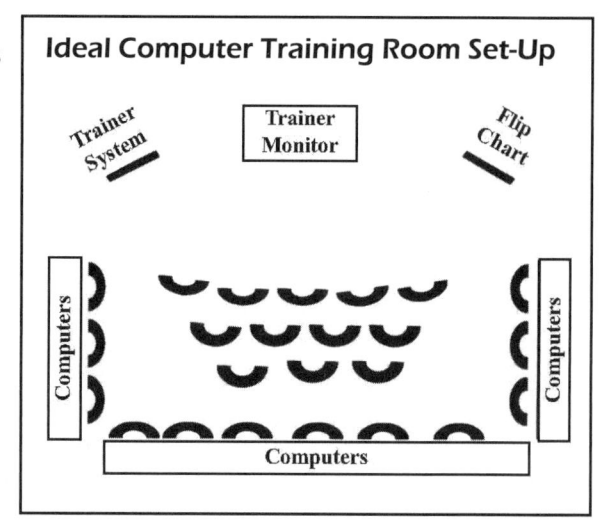

4. During practice sessions, the more experienced partner in the pair, when he has finished his practice, turns to the partner and offers help and assistance.

5. Chairs are set theatre-style in the middle of the room where participants gather to watch demonstrations or do partner revisits. Round tables set for groups of 4 or 5 may be substituted here if room size permits which would allow for small group discussions and interactions.

6. At each workstation, place the following tools: a nametag, a pen and highlighter, sticky notes, and a Koosh ball. A bandana should be taped to the top of the computer screen so that the user is able to drop the bandana and cover the screen when instructed to do so. (See Curtains Up, Curtains Down exercise in this book.)

http://bit.ly/CORETTCBT

CORE – Activities and Games for Technical Training

Variations: Alternate Computer Classroom Set-Up

Notice the following features of this room set-up:

1. The trainer's master system is set in the front of the room and controlled from the front left.

2. Participant computers are set in a classroom-style fashion with two systems set up on each table.

3. Participants are seated at the computers, each paired with another participant who is either more or less experienced at computer usage in general or in the use of the software being trained. (See Experience Line Up activity in this book.)

4. During practice sessions, the more experienced partner in the pair, when she has finished her practice, turns to the partner and offers help and assistance.

5. The trainer may have participants rotate in and out of the master system letting them control the master. The trainer states the instructions and watches the master system to make sure the participant there is correctly demonstrating what is being instructed. This frees up the trainer to move about the room and check for understanding and comprehension by other participants.

6. Each workstation should have the following tools: a nametag, a pen and highlighter, sticky notes, and a soft object for participants to pick up and hold (Koosh balls work great). A bandana should be taped to the top of the computer screen. (See Curtains Up, Curtains Down activity in this book).

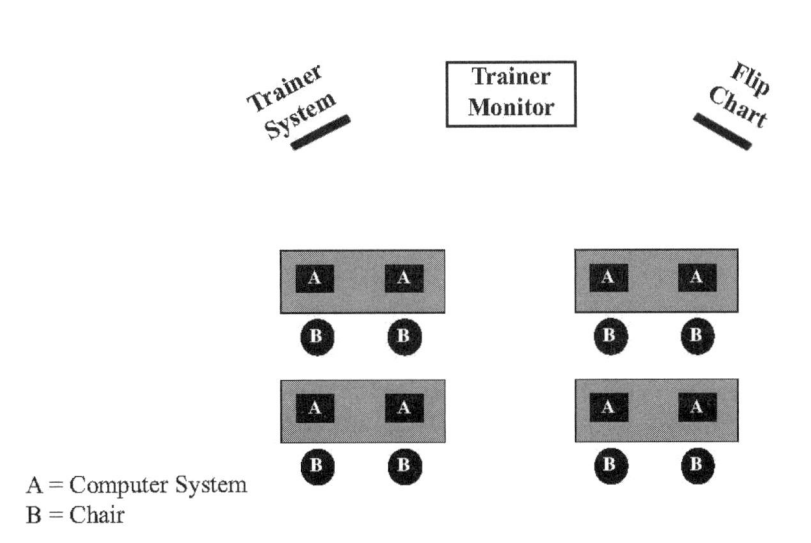

A = Computer System
B = Chair

CURTAINS UP, CURTAINS DOWN ☐ ☐ ☐

Author: Rich Meiss

Description: Give each participant a bandana to block the computer screen when not in use.

Objective: To avoid distraction by preventing participants from seeing their computer screens

Time: 5 minutes total class time

Audience: Any technical training audience learning at computers

Group Size: Any size, but usually a smaller group of 15 or fewer

Materials:
- Large bandanas
- Masking tape

Process:
1. Tape a large bandana to your master computer screen and then drape the bandana over the screen. As you begin the training class, tell participants that, from time to time, you are going to need their full attention on the master screen in the front of the room and, during those times, you are going to ask them to cover their computer screens.

2. Show them the model you've created on your screen.

3. Ask participants to pick up their bandanas along with some tape and tape the bandanas to their screens.

4. When you want the full attention of the group, the command you give is "curtains down." Participants then lower the bandanas over their screens so they are not visible to them. They should then pay attention to what is happening on the master screen. When it is time for them to practice, your command is then "curtains up." Participants may then raise their bandanas and continue to work on their computers.

Debrief: None

Variations: As a revisit technique, have participants all do a "curtains down" and revisit content in a creative way. For example, each participant may explain to a partner the key strokes that will lead them to the outcome they want to achieve, or participants may move to an open space in the room and actually do a "walk through" of the keystrokes. (See the related exercise in the Energizer section of this book called Keyboard Kinesthetics.)

Closers, Openers, Revisiters, Energizers

EXPERIENCE LINE-UP ☐ ☐ ☐

Author: Rich Meiss

Description: Have participants line up according to how much experience they have in your training topic.

Objective: To pair a more experienced participant with a lesser experienced one so he can provide guidance to his partner during practice exercises

Time: 5 minutes

Audience: Any training audience

Group Size: Usually a smaller training audience of fewer than 15

Materials: None

Process:
1. Ask everyone in the class to write down a number that represents the amount of time they've had experience with the topic of the day. For example, in an Excel class, participants should write down how many years they've been using Excel. Then ask the participants to form one single-file line in the front of the room with the less experienced on one side leading to the more experienced at the other end of the line. Once they have lined themselves up in this way, explain that you are now going to have them number off in a unique way to help create partnerships for the class.

2. In a group of 10, number the participants 1, 2, 3, 4, 5 – and then number the next five participants 1, 2, 3, 4, 5 as well. The numbered pairs (1s, 2s, etc.) will now form a partnership by sitting next to each other in the class.

3. Whenever the instructor assigns practice and application time, the more experienced person in the partnership should become a mentor to the other. For example, if one person completes the practice exercise, she should turn to her partner and ask if any help is needed. In this way, you get five additional "mini-instructors" in the course throughout the day, and it speeds up the process of the training. By doing it this way, you avoid the frustration that comes with having the most experienced person paired with the least experienced person.

Debrief: None

Variations: None

Closers, Openers, Revisiters, Energizers

GARAGE WINDOW

Author: Scott Enebo

Description: This is a brain teaser for paired partners.

Objective: To get a group thinking and working together to solve a problem and open up discussion for how content that is about to be covered will facilitate easier and more effective work or communication.

Time: 5 minutes

Audience: Any training audience

Group Size: Any

Materials: PowerPoint slide or flip chart paper

Process:
1. Show a slide or chart with the following description and question:

    "A homeowner had a single garage window. She decided to double the amount of light that came in while not changing the height or width of the window. The window measured 15 inches by 15 inches. She made four cuts to achieve her aim. How did she do it?"

2. Say, "Working with a partner, discuss possible solutions for how this could be done."

3. Allow time to discuss.

Note: You may wish to give more limitations on the problem stated above depending on your intent. To point learners in a more focused direction, let them know that:

   A. There are no curtains involved in this solution.

   B. There are no trees currently blocking the window.

   C. Cutting a second window is not an option for the homeowner. She can only work with the window currently in place.

4. Hear solutions.

5. If no one comes up with a solution, share the solution below.

Original Window — 15in. / 15in.

Four new cuts

CORE – Activities and Games for Technical Training

Debrief: If you wish to keep this brief, you may simply make a transition statement to share your purpose. One option might be, "What we are going to be talking about today is a lot like this puzzle. The tools and information that you are going to receive will not change your daily work dramatically, but they will help you be at least twice as effective if you follow the tips that we are going to share with you."

OR

If you would like to encourage your participants to think more critically about this, use these debrief questions:

1. What were your first reactions when you saw this puzzle?

2. What bits of information did you want to ignore in order to solve the problem?

3. When you saw the solution, what did you think about first?

4. How do the reactions of the group to this puzzle relate to the work we are currently doing?

5. How do you imagine this puzzle is a metaphor for what we are going to talk about today?

6. What would be the impact if we could not change our process (our height and width), but with a few minor changes, we could get twice the effectiveness (double the amount of light)?

Variations:
- Use this as a visual that you come back to throughout the course. In the original window, you can have participants write how things currently work or else describe the current process in place. As they go through the session, you can allow time to revisit content by having the learners fill in information in the new areas that have been cut away to capture the new insights that they are having.

- Use this as a closer by making a big visual of this window puzzle on the wall. Participants can write in action steps that they are going to take in the "new cuts" area, and then they can write the impact that this will have in the original window if they take these steps.

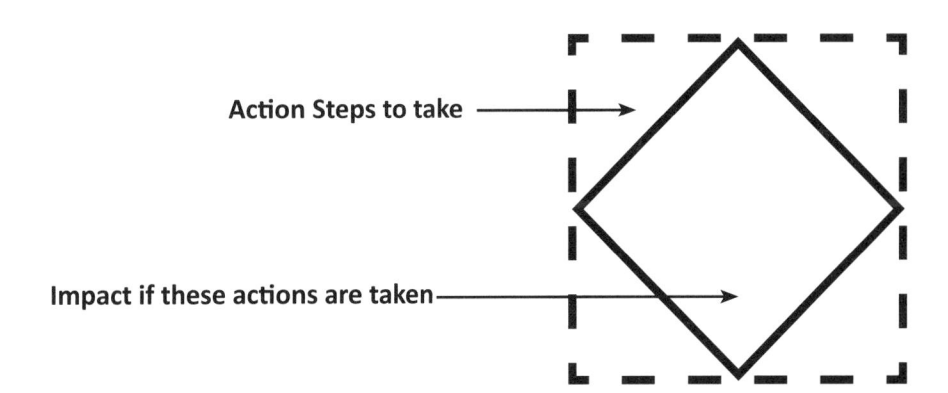

Action Steps to take

Impact if these actions are taken

Closers, Openers, Revisiters, Energizers

GET PUSSLED

Author: Marc Ratcliffe

Description: This is a simple but fun "find your partner" game which gets people moving.

Objective: Highlight the benefits of interaction and collaboration in problem solving

Time: 15 minutes

Audience: Any group

Group Size: Up to 12 people

Materials: Puzzle with one piece per participant

Process:
1. Create or purchase a basic puzzle with large pieces. Have enough pieces so every learner gets one.
2. Mix the puzzle pieces up and give one to each participant.
3. Explain that they have to find their partner who is someone with whom their puzzle piece connects. (To add an element of competition, prizes could be given out for those who found their partners first or who completed within a specified timeframe.)
4. Once the partners are found, instruct all the participants to work together to put all the pieces together to create a single picture.

Debrief: Use this activity to illustrate the importance of finding the right relationships in business or the right pegs for the right holes! Additionally, you could explore how success can be more effectively achieved through a systematic approach and collaboration with others. Most technical training involves the learning of systems and procedures, and this activity can help them start thinking about the "big picture" aspects of the session. The puzzle picture could also be used as a metaphor during your training.

Variations: A range of partnered objects could be used in place of puzzles.

Closers, Openers, Revisiters, Energizers

☐ ☐ ☐ IF YOU CAN DO THAT!
(MODIFIED POTATO AND STRAW EXERCISE)

Author: Rich Meiss

Description: Participants shove a plastic straw through a hard, raw potato.

Objective: To begin training with a high-energy activity and help those who struggle with "technophobia" realize they can learn technical content

Time: 10-12 minutes

Audience: Any training audience learning difficult or complex technical content

Group Size: Any size, but best if under 25 people

Materials:
- One raw, fairly good sized baker potato for every five participants
- Two average-sized, unwrapped, non-bendy drinking straws per person

Process: This exercise is a variation of a popular closing activity The Bob Pike Group has done for years in our Train-the-Trainer Boot Camps. A creative technical trainer saw us do this exercise and modified it into an opening exercise as follows.

1. Have several volunteers join you in the front of the room, form a single file line, and face the audience.

2. Give each participant a clean, raw potato and a regular-sized drinking straw.

3. Ask them, "How many of you believe you can shove this flimsy, plastic straw through this hard, raw potato?"

4. Usually several will be skeptical of their ability to do so. Ask the group if it is possible that some in the group are also skeptical of being able to learn how to use a computer, master the new software — insert whatever your day's objective is. Usually some will admit that they have some of those feelings. Ask them if they are willing to try, reminding the group that sometimes we just have to try new things even if we don't believe we can accomplish them.

5. Explain the process for doing the exercise. Have them hold the potato firmly in their non-dominant hand with a C clamp around the potato. This grip ensures that no fingers are on the bottom of the potato when a straw goes through.

   Then have them put the straw in their dominant hand, with their four fingers wrapped around the top part of the straw and their thumb firmly in place over the top. This traps the air and makes the straw rigid when it enters the potato.

6. Encourage them to practice the striking motion before they actually attempt the exercise. Have them raise their hands to about head level and then quickly plunge the straws downward, continuing the motion until the arms are extended at their sides. The key to the exercise is that they don't stop or pull back but follow through with a downward motion.

7. Tell them that, when they are ready, they should raise the straw and drive it through the potato, remembering to follow through. If they do not succeed the first time, give them a fresh straw and encourage them to try again. With some patience and encouragement on your part, everyone will be successful.

Debrief: Ask the group what this exercise might have to do with learning complex technical information or skills. The main point you want to make is that "if you can shove the straw through the potato, you probably also will be able to learn what we are teaching today." Tell them that if they trusted you to teach them this complex process, they should also trust you to teach them how to learn the material for the day. The goal is to remove the fear of trying and then jump into the learning.

Variations:
- If there is time and you have enough potatoes and straws, have the volunteers go and teach the other participants in a small group of four to five people how to do the exercise. You can then make the point that a part of the day will involve participants teaching each other content. One of the best ways to learn something new is to teach it to someone else.

- If you have a small group, you may wish to have enough potatoes and straws for everyone to do the activity together.

http://bit.ly/PotatoCloser

Closers, Openers, Revisiters, Energizers

LETTER SCRAMBLE

Author: Marc Ratcliffe

Description: Participants are given one letter of the alphabet and are to make words by grouping with other participants.

Objective: To get people moving early in the training session while building creativity and becoming more familiar with each other

Time: 20 minutes

Audience: Any training audience

Group Size: Any size

Materials: Cards with different letters of the alphabet on them (one per participant) with a mix of vowels and consonants.

Process:
1. Provide each participant with a card containing a single letter of the alphabet.

2. Tell the whole group their task is to arrange themselves into words using **all** the letters. The group can come up with a lot of words or just a few longer words but explain that every letter must be used.

3. After arranging themselves into these words, encourage the participants to introduce themselves to each other. It is important to have a good balance of vowels to consonants to give them the best chance of coming up with words quickly.

Debrief: The trainer should thank the participants for playing and remind them that in life they have to do the best with the cards they are dealt. However, by working together they can come up with a lot of different solutions.

Variations:
- As an extension, you could have a competition for which group can come up with the largest amount of different words.

- Instead of simply asking for groups of five, you could also use the activity as a means of forming groups during the session – e.g. "get into a five-letter word."

- You can also have the group come up with words that relate to the subject matter or topic of the session. Have some fun with this!

Closers, Openers, Revisiters, Energizers

MAP IT! ☐ ☐ ☐

Author: Karen Carlson

Description: Have participants practice giving directions to an activity.

Objective: To emphasize the importance of giving and following clear directions while showing how some people prefer visual directions and others prefer written or oral instructions

Time: 5-10 minutes

Audience: Any training audience

Group Size: Any

Materials:
- Paper
- Pens or markers

Process:
1. Have participants pair up.

2. Have Participant A give driving directions from one location like home to a second location like work to Participant B. Meanwhile, Participant B draws a map based on the directions given.

3. Once the map is drawn, the pair discusses the accuracy of the map and the ease or difficulty of following the provided directions.

4. Have the participants switch roles and repeat with Participant B giving the directions and Participant A drawing the map.

Debrief: Debrief with a discussion on the importance of giving clear directions or instructions for any exercise or task, as well as the possible consequences of steps that are skipped, missed, or performed incorrectly.

Variations: If room permits, Participant B may be blindfolded. Participant A gives directions from one point in the room to another point. Participant B listens and tries to find his way to the desired point. The importance of clear directions becomes even more evident when multiple pairs are doing this activity at the same time since the discussion in the room will become loud, making it harder for each blindfolded participant to hear his or her directions.

Closers, Openers, Revisiters, Energizers

NUTS & BOLTS

Author: Adrianne Roggenbuck

Description: Participants with a hardware nut scramble to find partners with the matching bolt.

Objective: Participants find their "nuts and bolts" partner and share their learning expectations for the course.

Time: 10 minutes

Audience: Technical group with some background knowledge of the content

Group Size: Best suited for groups up to 30 people. Even numbers work best for partnering purposes.

Materials: Pairs of nuts and bolts, enough so each participant gets either one nut or one bolt

Process:
1. Before class, count out an equal number of nuts and bolts to equal the number of participants.
2. Give each person either a nut or a bolt as they come in after a break or at the start of the session. You may want to give all nuts to one table and all bolts to another to ensure that the participants will mix.
3. Instruct participants to individually think about what the "nuts and bolts" of today's content might be.
4. Have them stand up and do a human scramble to find their "nuts and bolts" partner. Have them stand with their partner. Make sure every participant has only one partner.
5. Partners share what they think the "nuts and bolts" of the session will be for two minutes with each other.
6. Ask for volunteer "nuts" to share what their partnership discussed. Take as many volunteers as there are who have new or different information to share.
7. Thank the participants for sharing their expectations. Show them the agenda of topics for the session and indicate how their expectations do or do not line up.

Debrief: None

Variations: None

☐ ☐ ☐ ORIGINS OF EXPRESSIONS

Author: Priscilla Shumway

Description: Brainstorming the derivations of words or expressions

Objective: To get teams working together and networking to solve a puzzler. This illustrates the complexity of language as they begin to learn technical vocabulary.

Time: 10 minutes

Audience: Any technical training audience

Group Size: Any

Materials: Flip chart or PowerPoint slide

Process: Divide the group up into teams or pairs, depending on the size of the audience. Give them 2 minutes to brainstorm the derivation of the following words or expressions:

1. Scuba (diving)
2. Biscuit (snack food or cookie)
3. Put a sock in it (shut up)
4. Red tape (bureaucratic obstruction)
5. Bury the hatchet (agree to stop arguing)
6. Funny bone (upper arm bone)
7. Gander (to look at something enthusiastically)
8. Greenback (American dollar)

Answers:
1. **Scuba** (diving) — an acronym for 'self-contained underwater breathing apparatus.'

2. **Biscuit** (snack food) — from the Latin and French 'bis' (twice) and 'cuit' (baked); this is how biscuits were originally made, i.e., by baking twice.

3. **Put a sock in it** (shut up) — Invented in 1887, wind-up gramophones used a horn to amplify the sound from the needle on the record; the common way to control or limit the volume was to put a sock on the horn, thus muting the sound. The practice was still common in the 1930s.

4. **Red tape** (bureaucracy) — From the middle-to-late nineteenth century, the English custom for lawyers and government officials to tie documents together was with red tape. The term was first used metaphorically to describe official formality by Charles Dickens (1812-70).

5. **Bury the hatchet** (agree to stop arguing) — from the Native American custom, as required by their spirit gods, to bury all weapons out of sight while smoking the peace pipe.

6. **Funny bone** (upper arm bone) — a pun based on 'humerus,' the name of the upper arm bone.

7. **Gander** (to look at something enthusiastically) — an old English expression taken from the male goose craning its neck to look at something.

8. **Greenback** (American dollar) — from when the back side of banknotes issued during the Civil War were printed in green.

Debrief: What do the derivations of these terms tell us about the technical vocabulary we are learning? What are the derivations of some of our own technical terms and acronyms?

Variations: None

SEEK AND FIND ☐ ☐ ☐

Author: Priscilla Shumway

Description: Create a list of items participants need to find in a computer application while trying to beat the clock.

Objective: To preview a computer application which helps increase curiosity

Time: 10 minutes (can be modified to fit your training session)

Audience: Any technical training audience learning at computers

Group Size: Usually fewer than 15 people

Materials: Computers and appropriate software application

Process:
1. Provide the participants with five or six items to find or explore in a computer application. These can be written on a flip chart, in a handout, or on an electronic slide. Choose the most important tasks that you will be covering during this training session or the most common tasks they will be doing on the job.

2. Tell the participants how much time they will have to complete the scavenger hunt.

Debrief: Ask how many people found all of the items on the scavenger hunt. Which ones were more difficult to find? What questions arose for you as you hunted? How do you think you will use these items on the job?

Variations: Provide a handout that poses questions about the tasks such as "When using PowerPoint clip art, what selected media file types do you have to choose from?"

THINK OUTSIDE THE TRAINING ROOM BOX ☐ ☐ ☐

Author: Priscilla Shumway

Description: This checklist will help you as the trainer consider additional activities you can use to train technical content.

Objective: To create a list of appropriate out-of-classroom activities you can have your learners use to ensure better retention of technical material

Time: 15 minutes

Audience: Any technical training audience

Group Size: Any

Materials: Checklist

Process: Recent studies have shown that only 10 percent of training occurs in the classroom and that as much as 70 percent occurs on the job. This has often been referred to as GAAFOFY (Go Away And Find Out For Yourself). To determine if any portion of your technical training could be supported or better delivered through alternative activities, use this checklist to plan.

Activity	Person Responsible	Delivery Date
On the job coaching		
Interviewing other employees		
Reading assignments		
Attending internal briefings		
Lunch and learns		
e-Learning modules		
Customer visits		
Supplier/vendor visits		
Job shadow		
Assign to project team		
Field visit with mentor		
Site visits of other locations		
Trade shows and exhibits		
Shop floor and hands-on training		
Sister company visits		
Other		

Debrief: None

Closers, Openers, Revisiters, Energizers

TRUE/FALSE ANTICIPATION GUIDE

Author: Adrianne Roggenbuck

Description: Participants complete a true/false quiz based on the content to be covered.

Objective: To determine each participant's level of knowledge on the day's topic

Time: 10 minutes

Audience: Any technical training audience

Group Size: Works best with groups up to 15 people but could be adapted for larger groups if they are subdivided into table teams of 4-6 people

Materials: True/False handout

Process:
1. Hand out the T/F Anticipation Guide.

2. Give participants 3½ minutes to individually circle T or F for each statement.

3. Once participants have completed the guide, have them stand up and circulate around the room to compare their answers with each other for another 3 minutes (also known as a "human scramble"). They may change their answers based on what they hear from other people. At the end of 3 minutes, have them sit down.

4. Poll the group on each sentence to see how many responded correctly, but do not tell them if the sentence is true or false. This will give you a good indication of the knowledge level of the group.

Debrief: Tell the participants that they will be verifying their answers throughout the day. When they have verified the answer, they will record where or when that verification occurred by listing either a page number in their manual or the time of day in the third column of their handout. (This will help keep participants engaged and make them more responsible for their own learning.) At the end of the training, go back to the guide and share the correct responses and where or when the verification occurred.

Variations:
- For a larger group, allow participants to discuss their answers with the others at their table instead of doing a human scramble.

- Call attention to the guide after you have verified each statement.

- Allow participants to compare and share their verifications at various points during the training instead of waiting until the end.

True/False Anticipation Guide		
Statement	T/F	Verification
1.	T/F	
2.	T/F	
3.	T/F	
4.	T/F	
5.	T/F	
6.	T/F	
7.	T/F	
8.	T/F	
9.	T/F	
10.	T/F	

REVISITERS

Interval reinforcement is one of the best gifts you can give your students and one of the best ways to maximize content retention. In his research, Albert Mehrabian determined that a person exposed to an idea six times over the course of a month would retain greater than 90 percent of the information learned after one month. Expose your learners to content one time? Mehrabian found retention is less than 10 percent after 30 days. This is why we suggest revisiting content six times in different ways over the course of your class and using follow-up techniques after.

Unfortunately, most learning events today cover ideas one time and expect the participants to remember them. Maybe the reason this happens is that trainers believe it is boring to repeat themselves over and over. But doing a revisit doesn't have to be boring. Creative trainers find interesting ways to allow the participants to do the revisit, thus making it more interesting and effective. So here's the key: review is when the trainer does it, and revisit is when the participants do it. Therein lies the power – getting the participants to revisit.

Here are some tips for helping participants retain more from your sessions:

- Revisit early and often. Remember, we need to cover key content at least six times for maximum retention.

- Don't call it "review." In our sessions, we suggest trainers avoid the "R" word (review) and instead use the word "revisit." The difference is that the instructor is the one who usually does a review, covering the content again, while in a revisit, the participants are going over the content another time in a more interesting way.

- Use a variety of revisit techniques. This keeps the interest level of participants high and helps them stay engaged in the learning process.

The following pages contain some of our favorite revisiting techniques for technical training. Each is very powerful. Enjoy learning and employing these techniques, knowing that ultimately your learners will be the ones to benefit!

http://bit.ly/CORETTRevisit

Closers, Openers, Revisiters, Energizers

BUYERS AND SELLERS ☐ ☐ ☐

Author: Marc Ratcliffe

Description: This is a revisiting activity where participants have to reflect upon the session to determine the most important content for them and why. In sharing with others, they will have to persuasively explain and substantiate their position. They will also have the opportunity to be persuaded by others and will ultimately be able to add to their own list based on the responses from other participants.

Objective: Identify key content to put into practice post-training.

Time: 10-15 minutes

Audience: Any

Group Size: Any size

Materials:
- Pens
- Paper

Process:
1. Provide each participant with a sheet of paper and ask them to fold it in half.

2. Instruct them to write "Buy" on one side and "Sell" on the other side.

3. Next, encourage participants to consider all the content covered in the session and identify the most important points or topics for them. Try to limit this to two or three items. This should be written in the "Sell" section. Explain that they will have to justify why these were so key during a later sharing with others in the group. At this stage, ask them to leave the "Buy" section blank until further notice.

4. Once the participants have completed their "Sell" section, explain they are about to enter an "Ideas Market" where they can buy and sell the best ideas from the day. They will use the points listed in their "Sell" section to share with others and should add anything they like from their peers in the "Buy" section.

5. Ask if there is anything you can clarify, then tell them to try selling their items to two or three people.

Debrief: Once the time has concluded, bring the group back together and take a selection of the best ideas captured. Explain that people will not always buy into our ideas, and we have to be persuasive to bring them around. Additionally, it will be important to point out that some of the best ideas can come from others which can be the beauty of collaboration.

Variations: As an extension, the activity could be concluded on the job where participants have to return to their workplaces to try to "sell" the ideas from the session as well as bring back or "buy" new ideas not covered in class.

Closers, Openers, Revisiters, Energizers

☐ ☐ ☐ CLASS REPLAY

Author: Scott Enebo

Description: In most major sports, the use of instant replay has made it easier for an audience to fully understand what happened. In this strategy, we take this concept into the classroom to help learners look at information again as needed from different angles and at different speeds.

Objective: To create a structure that will allow learners to revisit and review content in meaningful detail

Time: 15 minutes

Audience: Any training audience

Group Size: 6-30 people

Materials: Index cards or sticky notes

Process:
1. Say, "As you know, when we watch sports, there are times when it is necessary to use instant replay to fully grasp what just happened. We are going to bring instant replay into this class as we take a look at some of the concepts that we covered but would like to look at again in greater detail.

    "In just a moment, you and your table are going to have 2 minutes to brainstorm any pieces of content that you think would be helpful to review in some sort of detail. You will write each of these ideas on a separate index card. With it, you will tell how you would like to see the information reviewed. For example, you may want: [write the bolded information on a flip chart]

    a. **Slo-Mo** – Take the concept and slow it down in order to review steps in greater detail,

    b. **Alternate Angle** – Sometimes we cannot see everything from the angle presented so take the same content and look at it in a new way,

    c. **Reverse** – To make sure that the information is completely absorbed, look at the information in the opposite order, or

    d. **Fast Forward** – This is great for when you think you have the concept but you want to go over it quickly one more time.

    Please be specific on exactly what you would like to look at again. What may I clarify?"

2. Set a timer and let table groups write.

3. Ask table groups to select the card with the topic that needs the most clarification.

4. Say, "When I say go, we are going to pass the idea that you just selected to the table next to you. The card that you receive will be the one for which you will now be responsible. You will read the content that should be revisited and the way in which the group would like it. Your group will then have 3 minutes to prepare how you will present this information back to the group, being sure to incorporate the request for how to share it back [slo-mo, alternate angle, reverse, fast forward]. What questions do you have before we begin?"

5. Set the timer for 3 minutes.

6. After time is up, have groups share back with the rest of the class. Feel free to fill in ideas or concepts that are left out to ensure that everything is covered.

Debrief: This revisit does not require a debrief as the act of sharing content is the real power in the activity. It helps encourage learners to fully own the information covered, which will make it easier to implement back on the job.

Variations:
- Feel free to take this idea up a notch. Give each table a red flag. Let the tables know that, at any time, they can throw this flag to ask for an instant replay according to the same criteria above. This can create a fun atmosphere and helps to cultivate an environment where learners take responsibility for their own learning.

- Instead of using this as a revisit technique, make this into a closing activity. Instead of teach-back ideas, learners will write down their thoughts to questions like:

    – What is something that you would slow down?

    – What would you zoom in on from today?

    – What would make the highlight reel for you?

  Ask learners to share back what they wrote with a partner or with the entire group.

Closers, Openers, Revisiters, Energizers

COMMAND KEEPER REVISIT ☐ ☐ ☐

Author: Rich Meiss

Description: Each member of the learning group is assigned a different command associated with the learning content such as the "save" command. Each person is then responsible for revisiting the information on that command whenever that command comes up in training.

Objective: To make "dry and boring" content come to life with this revisit technique

Time: 10-15 minutes

Audience: Any technical training audience

Group Size: 15 or less

Materials: None

Process:
1. Pick out the different commands or aspects of a technical training topic.

2. As participants come into the room, assign each of them a different command. In a computer training class, for example, one person would be in charge of the "save" command.

3. Whenever that process is covered in the training, have the assigned person jump up and tell how the process works or have him demonstrate the procedure.

4. Rotate the keeper of the commands to different participants thus keeping the attention and interest of the entire group. In this way, several revisits of the key components can be covered at various times throughout the day.

Debrief: A final debrief of the commands can be done at the end of the training day.

Variations: This process could be used for a variety of different training programs. In sales training, for example, as each step of the sales process is taught, someone could be assigned to be the "keeper" of that step of the process. Then at various times throughout the day, the instructor could ask, "What's the purpose of the demonstration step?" The keeper of that step would then jump up and give the answer. In addition to being a good revisit of content, this process can serve as an energizer during a long day of training.

Closers, Openers, Revisiters, Energizers

COMPUTER APPLICATION WINDOW PANE ☐ ☐ ☐

Author: Priscilla Shumway

Description: The trainer creates a window pane graphic with visual depictions of a process.

Objective: To help learners revisit and retain the steps in a process from a computer application

Time: 20 minutes

Audience: Any technical training audience

Group Size: Any

Materials: Flip chart paper

Process:
1. Draw a window pane with one pane for each step in the process. Do not use more than nine panes.

2. In each pane, replicate the keyboard key or icon from the application that represents the step in the process.

3. Below or above each icon, write in two or three words that represent that step. Try to use the same terminology as is used in the application.

4. Explain each step in the process as you draw the window pane. Revisit the steps and ask the participants to repeat the words to that step.

Debrief: None

Variations: As an additional revisit activity, provide a partially filled out window pane and ask the participants to fill in the missing icons and terms.

Inserting a photograph into a PowerPoint slide

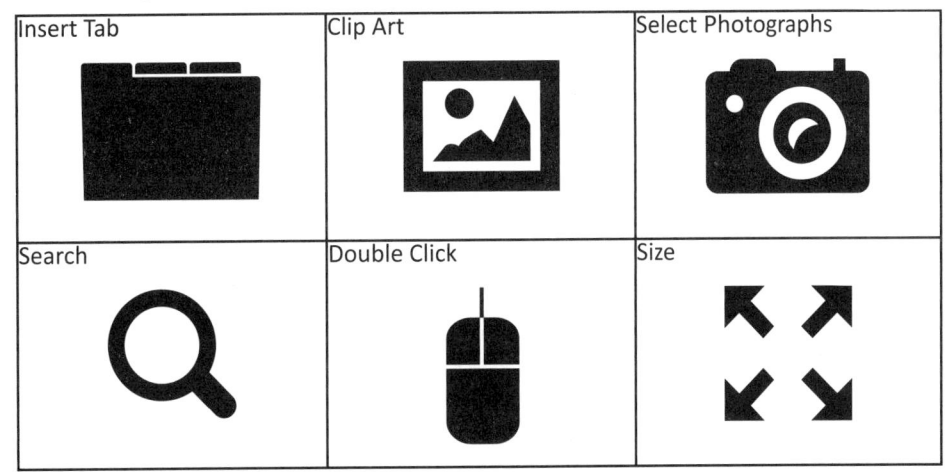

Insert Tab	Clip Art	Select Photographs
Search	Double Click	Size

Closers, Openers, Revisiters, Energizers

COMPUTER QUIZ CAROUSEL

Author: Adrianne Roggenbuck

Description: Learners create questions for other learners as all learners move from computer to computer (as on a carousel) to answer the questions.

Objective: To assess knowledge of content previously delivered

Time: 15 minutes

Audience: Any technical training audience in a computer lab

Group Size: Any size group, as the questions are generated individually

Materials: Computer with Internet access for each participant

Process:

1. Subdivide the larger group and assign a segment of content to each smaller group or individual. Participants generate two to three review questions covering key concepts for their assigned segment of content and type them into their computers. Encourage them to create questions that start with why, how, or where. This will restrict the number of yes/no questions generated.

2. When the questions are completed, have participants move to the computer to their right and type in the answers to as many questions as they can in two minutes. Then have them move to the next computer and allow them two minutes again to read the answers already written and add to or refine them.

3. Continue the carousel until all content areas have been covered. Participants then return to their own computers.

4. Each participant checks the answers to the questions that he or she generated and presents any misconceptions or errors to the large group.

5. Questions and answers are then emailed to the instructor for final inspection and may be used to generate an assessment for a future class.

Debrief: Thank the group for their participation and ask them to email their documents to you.

Variations: This activity may be used at the end of each segment of content rather than waiting until all of the content has been delivered.

Closers, Openers, Revisiters, Energizers

CREATE YOUR OWN JOB AID ☐ ☐ ☐

Author: Karen Carlson

Description: Participants create their own job aids for the content learned in class.

Objective: For participants to develop a practical job aid for them and their team to assist in the transition to the new task/process/application

Time: 5-10 minutes

Audience: Any training audience

Group Size: Any

Materials: Writing instruments or computers

Process: Have participants discuss the steps of a process covered in class to determine what information should be included on the job aid. Using paper or a computer, have each person develop his own job aid to assist his team in learning this new application.

Debrief: Once everyone has completed his job aid, the group then reviews one another's job aids, asks questions and adds content as needed to ensure that the job aid is clear and complete. The facilitator may opt to print or laminate the job aids or post them on the company's intranet for easy access.

Variations: None

FOCUS GROUP ☐ ☐ ☐

Author: Marc Ratcliffe

Description: This is an activity that could be modified for any subject area. Essentially, the trainer provides the participants with a list of suggested topics to discuss selected from the subject matter of the session; they will present this bite-sized content back to the group in a creative fashion.

The Focus Group promotes interactivity, helps to reinforce information and engages the group as it gives them ownership over the material. Further, it changes the focus from the trainer to the participant, and the diversity of vocal and presentation styles makes for a more interesting session. It works well after a break as it gets the group focused but in a relaxing and fun way.

Objective: To bring creativity to traditionally dry, technical content and encourage collaboration to promote reinforcement of content.

Time: 45 minutes

Audience: Any technical training audience

Group Size: 20 or fewer people

Materials:
- Flip chart paper
- Pens
- Other creative items to support presentations

Process:
1. Divide the participants into smaller groups of between three and five persons and provide them with a list of topics relevant to the day's session.

2. The participants should then be asked to select one of the topics for their exclusive discussion and focus.

3. Each group will then work with its selected topic for about 20-25 minutes and come up with a summary response to present back to the rest of the class. Encourage a creative presentation of the topics which could include, but is not limited to: posters, music/rhymes, role plays, PowerPoint presentations and, for those who are most daring, an interpretive dance! You could choose to provide a prize to the most creative group to engage some wholesome competition.

Debrief: Celebrate the successes of the participants' creativity and summarize their pertinent points. As necessary, you can expand upon points from the presentation.

Variations: This activity could be easily transformed for online learning where individual participants could be charged with a small part of content that they have to share with a group of other online learners. These participants could be given the choice of web-based or app-based software to create their focused presentation. Once completed, these presentations could be made available online for the ongoing resource of all present and future participants in the relevant program.

☐ ☐ ☐ "LABEL THIS" RELAY

Author: Becky Pike Pluth

Description: This takes any technical drawing, document or process and allows the learners to work together to label parts of the system or process together in a physical way.

Objective: To provide a kinesthetic way to ensure all learners are understanding and comprehending the content covered

Time: 5-15 minutes

Audience: Any training audience

Group Size: 2-35 people

Materials:
- One wall poster for each group. The poster should have a technical drawing already on it complete with blank lines so participants can label the various parts.
- Markers
- Chime (optional)
- Upbeat music (optional)

Process:

1. Hang the posters backward on the wall so participants cannot see the drawing. Make sure the tape can be reversed once the activity has begun.

2. Say, "In just a moment, I will say, 'Go.' You will take a marker from your table and find a group of 3-4 people to work with. Then go to one of the posters on the wall and await further instructions. Mark, set, go!"

3. Wait for all groups to gather at the wall. Optional: ring a chime to get their attention.

4. Say, "Thank you for listening. You are about to participate in a relay race against the other teams. On the opposite side of the poster in front of you is an image of _____ (fill in the blank with what it is: a screenshot of a system, a fork lift, etc.). Your group should stand three feet from the poster and then, one at a time, go to the poster and fill in a blank as quickly as possible. Keep rotating until all the blanks are filled. If you are in line and know an answer, you can help your teammates recall the information. When your group has all of the blanks filled in, do a group shout out to let us know you are done! The winning team is the team done first. What may I clarify?"

5. Clarify any questions.

6. Say, "On your mark, get set, go!"

7. Optional: turn on upbeat music. (For affordable, royalty-free music, visit The Bob Pike Group website at http://bit.ly/trainingmusic.) Turn the music off when a group finishes.

Debrief: Have all learners go to the winning group's poster and have the winners share their answers with the whole group. Correct anything necessary along the way reminding the group that you said the first team done wins, not the first one with all the correct answers!

Variations: Use this as an opener. On a PowerPoint slide, put all the answers to the fill-ins. Tell the group that it is their job to attempt to place all of these labels in the correct place on the poster. Although you haven't covered the content yet, it is an easy way to introduce the concepts. After a group finishes, the debrief becomes the lecture. Have everyone meet at the first group's poster and share about the different labels from that part of the room. After the lecture, they can go back to their workbooks and fill in their diagrams.

☐ ☐ ☐ MAGNET WORD SUMMARY

Author: Adrianne Roggenbuck

Description: This revisiting activity would be done either after participants have read some information or after a segment of content. Participants are summarizing the key points they have read or heard about. This gets them to revisit key information and synthesize it, which enhances retention and recall.

Objective: To identify the key words associated with a key concept and write a short summary

Time: 10 minutes

Audience: Any training audience

Group Size: Any size, as this is done with a partner or a small group

Materials: Magnet Word template

Process:
1. Divide the group into partnerships or small groups of three to five people. Distribute the Magnet Word template. This may be done either electronically or in hard copy.
2. Instruct the partners to search through the information they just read (or heard) to identify one key concept that they will use as their Magnet Word. It could be a single word or a phrase. Explain that a magnet word attracts information that is important to the topic just like a magnet.
3. After selecting the magnet word or phrase, partners will write as many keywords as they can that relate to it on the Magnet Word template. The magnet word should be written in large bold letters in the center and the keywords are written around the magnet word in smaller letters.
4. These keywords will then be used to write a brief summary of one to three sentences at the bottom of the template.
5. The completed Magnet Word summaries will then be shared with the whole group.

Debrief: None

Variations:
- This activity could be done on chart paper rather than on the template and a gallery walk afterward would be an ideal way to share what each partnership created.
- To ensure that there are no duplications, topic areas could be assigned to each group or partnership.

MAGNET WORD SAMPLE

Interactive   content-related

fun

curiosity

Opener

Breaks preoccupation

Self-esteem

Nametags   human scramble

Goal Writing

SUMMARY:

An opener is a fun, interactive, content-related activity used to break preoccupation and raise participants' curiosity level. It should always be used to raise or maintain participants' self-esteem. A few examples are: Nametags, Human Scramble, and Goal Writing.

Closers, Openers, Revisiters, Energizers

MAGNET WORD SUMMARY

_____

SUMMARY:

Permission granted by the authors of CORE Activities and Games for Technical Training to reproduce this page.

NAME THAT PART ☐ ☐ ☐

Author: Rich Meiss

Description: On a diagram, participants name the parts of a piece of equipment. The trainer then calls out the "part number" and participants name that item.

Objective: To create a review process to learn about equipment

Time: 5-10 minutes

Audience: Learners in any technical training session

Group Size: Any size

Materials: Worksheets with a picture of the equipment to be labeled

Process:
1. Create a worksheet that has a drawing or picture of a piece of equipment with the various parts of the equipment numbered.

2. After teaching about the equipment, hand out the worksheets and ask participants to name the parts. They can do this either individually or as part of a team.

3. After participants have had time to name the parts, call out the part number and ask them to state the name. Go through all the parts in this manner.

Debrief: Do a final debrief, naming all the parts taught during the session.

Variations:
- Enlarge the worksheet into a poster, creating enough posters so that each small group can have its own poster. Create a set of numbered sticky notes and a sheet with descriptions of each of the part's functions. Give each group a poster, a set of sticky notes, and a descriptive sheet. Ask them to place the numbered sticky note by its corresponding correct part. If you have multiple diagrams, you can then switch teams to other posters and repeat the process. Posters can then be displayed in the room for further reinforcement throughout the training process.

- Or, as a variation on this variation, have participants in the first round correctly label their chart, EXCEPT FOR THREE LABELS that are deliberate mistakes. Each group rotates to a new chart where they find and fix the errors.

RACE TO THE FINISH ☐ ☐ ☐

Author: Priscilla Shumway

Description: After pulling out mixed-up steps of a process from an envelope, teams race to put together a process correctly.

Objective: To reinforce and revisit specific steps in a technical process

Time: 5 minutes

Audience: Any training audience

Group Size: Any size in groups of 4-6 people

Materials: One envelope per group. In the envelope is every step in a process written on individual slips of paper that are then shuffled.

Process:
1. Provide each table with an envelope with all of the steps to the process.

2. Say, "When I say go, open your envelopes and put the steps to the XYZ process into the correct order. The first team to do this correctly is the winner."

3. Allow the teams to race until one team has finished. However, the trainer should verify that they have done it correctly before declaring them the winner.

4. Allow all teams to finish. Winners may help other teams if desired.

Debrief: None

Variations: At a later time in the training, randomly hand out the steps in the process on slips of paper to different participants and ask them to come and stand in the front of the room in the correct order. Have the audience correct them if needed.

Closers, Openers, Revisiters, Energizers

TECHNICAL TERM TRIP UP

Author: Priscilla Shumway

Description: Ever played "Dictionary"? In this version, the trainer calls out a technical term. Participants write down their best guesses as to the meaning while the trainer writes down the correct one. Then they all vote on which description is the correct one.

Objective: To create a review process to learn specialized, technical vocabulary terms

Time: 5 minutes

Audience: Learners in any technical training session

Group Size: Any size

Materials: Index cards

Process:
1. Give each participant several index cards.
2. Call out one of the technical or specialized vocabulary terms from the training class.
3. Ask the participants to write their definition of the term on one index card along with their initials.
4. You write the official definition from the manual on a card.
5. Collect the index cards, shuffle them and read all of the definitions. Each participant votes for the definition he or she thinks is the one from the manual.
6. Scoring:
   - one point for correctly guessing the manual definition
   - one point for the participant each time someone votes for his or her definition

Debrief: Do a final debrief revisiting all of the correct definitions.

Variations: None

Closers, Openers, Revisiters, Energizers

WHAT'S WRONG WITH THIS PICTURE? ☐ ☐ ☐

Author: Karen Carlson

Description: Participants team up and look at a screenshot filled with correct and incorrect data and work to correct the misinformation.

Objective: To reinforce processes already covered by having participants pinpoint incorrect information

Time: 5-10 minutes

Audience: Software training participants

Group Size: Any

Materials: Copies of various screenshots showing correct and incorrect data (each pair should have a different screenshot). Be sure to include both correct data and incorrect data in the screenshot.

Process:
1. Have participants team up.
2. Give each team a copy of a different worksheet that shows a screenshot of a data entry form or other applicable screen covered in class.
3. Participants work in pairs to analyze their screenshot and spot correct and incorrect data. For incorrect data, participants jot down the correct data for that field.

Debrief: Each pair shares their analysis with the group, especially highlighting the areas they corrected.

Variations: Various screenshots can be put on posters and hung throughout the training room. Pairs can then travel the room to mark one correct and one incorrect data point per poster. When time is called, pairs stop at the poster nearest them and report out the key points. The group adds comments about additional points that need to be addressed on that poster. The facilitator then verifies completeness and accuracy of each poster.

WHICH COMES FIRST?

Author: Karen Carlson

Description: Teams work together to put the steps of a process in the correct order while eliminating unnecessary steps.

Objective: To visually illustrate the correct order of steps in a process while gauging participants' retention

Time: 5-7 minutes, depending on the number of steps in the process

Audience: Any technical training audience

Group Size: Any, preferably at least one participant per step in the process

Materials: A list of steps printed out on cards or 8.5"x11" paper, one step per card or piece of paper

Process:
1. Have participants get together in small groups.
2. Provide each group with a set of cards describing the process being taught. Include some extra, unnecessary steps that would slow down the process.
3. Have the teams work together to line up the process in the correct order while eliminating any unnecessary steps.

Debrief: Verify that groups lined up the process in the correct order. Ask the group which steps they determined were unnecessary or would slow down the process and why. Is there a reason some of those steps might still need to be part of the process or can they truly be eliminated?

Variations: This could also be done for software or data entry applications where the groups discuss and number the correct steps in completing that application.

ENERGIZERS

MENTAL STIMULATORS and PHYSICAL ACTIVATORS

Great presentations and training sessions keep participants energized through the use of effective presentation methods as well as mental stimulators and physical energizers. This section of the CORE book offers a variety of energizers to keep participants active and engaged. Energizers are useful throughout a session and probably are most useful during these times: after lunch, after a break, when the room temperature is too warm, and during the middle of a long content presentation.

Make sure to use these types of activities purposefully and strategically. The audience should have a sense of why you are doing them. Using simple statements such as "Okay, let's get our minds focused back on the learning process by starting with this simple quiz," or "Let's wake up our brains this afternoon by examining this trivia test" will help participants understand why you are doing the activity or exercise. And, while energizers are not required to tie into the content, many of these activities do, so if you are looking for more revisiting ideas or openers, don't forget to look through here, too!

This section contains both mental stimulators and physical energizers. The mental stimulators create "mental sparks" that stimulate the brain and keep participants ready to learn. This set of activities includes trivia tests, storytelling, and activities that are larger than life! Mental stimulators are useful after breaks or after lunch as a way to re-focus the group on the topic at hand or to stimulate the brain and get participants back into a learning mood.

When used correctly, mental stimulators literally create energy in the group. You can see the physical energy increase through the mental stimulation. The activities included here are easy to use. Copy them and hand them out to participants or read them to the group at appropriate times.

Physical activators get the body moving. These activities are often simple, competitive and fun. They range from things like musical chairs to kinesthetics. Some of these physical activators are also designed to be controlled stretch breaks. That is, they involve some questions or activities that can be related to the session content, thus creating a double win – a stretch for the participants while communicating a learning point.

When used correctly, physical activators will get participants back into a learning mood with a refreshed body and a re-focused mind. Although many of these are not content-related, most participants will make the connection between the activity and the purpose for which it was intended – to help the learning process. Enjoy these new energizers!

http://bit.ly/CORETTEnergizers

CAN YOU TOP THIS?

Author: Adrianne Roggenbuck

Description: Participants try to top each other's stories about technology gone wrong.

Objective: To generate enthusiasm around sharing participants' worst technology horror stories

Time: 5-7 minutes, depending on how many stories are shared

Audience: Any technical training audience

Group Size: Any size group subdivided into teams of 4-5 people

Materials: None

Process:
1. Ask participants to close their eyes for a moment and envision the worst technology snafu that has ever happened to them. When they have decided on one, have them stand up.

2. Once everyone is standing, have them sit once again and share their horror stories at their tables. Have each table team select one story they think is the absolute worst. The person whose story gets selected will be the spokesperson for the team.

3. You begin the sharing with one of your own technology horror stories, and then say, "Can you top this?"

4. Ask for a volunteer spokesperson to share their story. After they finish their story, you say, "Can you top that?"

5. Continue the same process with the stories until no one else volunteers to share.

Debrief: We have all had technology issues that have negatively impacted our effectiveness. If we are aware of the possible pitfalls and have more than one way to solve a problem, then we are more likely to recover more quickly from the negative occurrence.

Variations: Add a discussion of how the issues were resolved if you have 10-15 minutes for the activity instead of 5-7 minutes.

Closers, Openers, Revisiters, Energizers

FACE TO FACE

Author: Becky Pike Pluth

Description: Learners find a partner and follow the directions such as "back to back" as quickly as possible in this race against time.

Objective: To get blood moving and increase the energy in the room

Time: 1-5 minutes

Audience: Any technical training audience. For those in a computer-based classroom, the variation below will be more applicable.

Group Size: 8 or more people

Materials: None

Process:
1. For this exercise, you need an odd number of participants. Have everyone in the classroom find a partner and stand face-to-face, except for you. You, as the facilitator, are the only one without a partner. If you have even numbers with you participating, you will demonstrate and then not participate in the actual exercise.

2. Say, "When I call 'face-to-face' or 'back to back,' everyone needs to find a new partner and stand either facing one another or stand back-to-back. If you do not find a partner, you become the leader. You will now call face-to-face, back-to-back, hand-to-hand, or elbow-to-elbow."

3. Demonstrate this one time with the group so that they get the idea.

4. After several changes, you can end the exercise. The energy will be back up, blood will be flowing optimally to the brain, and learners will be ready to reengage.

Debrief: None

Variations:
- If in a computer-based classroom, try this modification. Have everybody find a partner. As the leader, you shout out the instructions and they follow them. You might first say "face-to-face" and then follow that up with "elbow to knee." You can award points for groups that complete the exercise first or you can just do several in quick succession and the learners will be ready to reengage.

- You can also take the learners out of the classroom for a brief break and take them outside. While outside, they become individual participants. You can now do things like elbow to bench, back to tree, bottom to grass, etc. This not only gives you a field trip outside but a fun, quick way to enjoy the outdoors.

http://bit.ly/CORETTF2F

Closers, Openers, Revisiters, Energizers

☐ ☐ ☐ I FOUGHT THE LAW

Author: Scott Enebo

Description: When systems or processes change, it can be hard to accept the changes or to understand why things are the way they are. To help get people ready for change, share some outdated laws or rules that are still on state law books today.

Objective: To help people overcome resistance to the changes that are being implemented

Time: 5-10 minutes

Audience: Any training audience

Group Size: Any

Materials: Handout with laws printed or PowerPoint slides

Process:
1. Give participants a handout of the laws on the following page (use fewer of these laws to match your time) or else incorporate them into a PowerPoint deck.
2. Ask learners to work with a partner and decide whether each of the laws is "True" or "False." In other words, is this a law that is still on the books or is it made up?

    Note: All of the laws listed are real laws. They may seem silly, but these are laws enacted by states for reasons that are no longer fully known.
3. Complete as many of these as time allows.
4. Review the answers with the participants. Hear their guesses first and then share the correct answer. Do the first several and once it is becoming clear that all of these are real laws, tell the class that these are all actual laws.

Debrief:
1. Looking at this list, which laws seem the most believable? The most outrageous?
2. Which of these laws would you find challenging to obey?
3. Why are some rules or changes that happen around us easier to accept than others?
4. Where have you seen disregard for rules or change in your life?
5. What are some examples from work where rules were ignored or change was resisted?
6. What would be helpful for us to know as we are looking at making these upcoming changes?

Variations:
- Write each of the real laws from this activity on a strip of paper. Ask participants to come up with laws that they think would be ridiculous to enact and write them on similar strips of paper. Begin drawing out these strips and reading them to the class and ask them to decide whether they are real or made up. To make this a visual process, have participants stand up and move to one side of the room if they think the law is real and to the other side of the room if they believe it to be fake.

- Research some of these laws and then give the backstory to a few of them. This will help clarify that there is always a reason as to why it exists. Ask participants to then consider the rules or regulations being discussed and come up with their own thoughts on why they think they came into existence and why they are important to learn and follow.

	Law
True or False	In California, no person shall wear a mask or disguise on a public street without a permit from the sheriff.
True or False	Colorado prohibits the use of rain barrels to catch rain as the rain has been legally allocated to the state and the individual may not use water to which he/she does not have rights.
True or False	In New Orleans, Fire Code outlaws the cursing of firefighters while they are in the performance of their duties.
True or False	In North Carolina, it is illegal to hold more than two sessions of bingo per week, and those sessions may not exceed 5 hours each session.
True or False	State code deems it unlawful in West Virginia for any person to have in his possession or to display any red or black flag.
True or False	A United States federal law makes it illegal to issue a fake Weather Bureau forecast.
True or False	In Kentucky, a female shall not appear in a bathing suit on any highway within this state.
True or False	A state law in Mississippi prohibits the seduction of a female over the age of eighteen by promised or pretended marriage.
True or False	In Youngstown, Ohio, you may not run out of gas.
True or False	In Tennessee, no person may import or possess any type of live skunk, or to sell, barter, exchange any live skunk, except bona fide zoological parks.
True or False	In Minnesota a person may not cross state lines with a duck atop his head.
True or False	In Wisconsin it is illegal to kiss on a train.
True or False	Women must obtain written permission from their husbands to wear false teeth in Vermont.
True or False	Kisses may last for no more than five minutes in Iowa.
True or False	In North Dakota, beer and pretzels can't be served at the same time in any bar or restaurant.
True or False	You may not have an ice cream cone in your back pocket at any time in Alabama.
True or False	Billboards are outlawed in Hawaii.
True or False	In Alaska, moose may not be viewed from an airplane.
True or False	Hunting camels is prohibited in Arizona.
True or False	In Arkansas, alligators may not be kept in bathtubs.
True or False	In order for a pickle to officially be considered a pickle, it must bounce in Connecticut.
True or False	If an elephant is left tied to a parking meter, the parking fee has to be paid just as it would for a vehicle in Florida.
True or False	In Idaho, it is a crime to ride a merry-go-round on Sundays.
True or False	It is illegal to drive a camel on the highway in Nevada.
True or False	In Mississippi, vagrancy is punishable by either 30 days in prison or a $250 fine.
True or False	In Louisiana, rituals that involve the ingestion of blood, urine, or fecal matter are not allowed.
True or False	You may not catch a fish by any body part except the mouth in Pennsylvania.
True or False	Road kill may be taken home for supper in West Virginia.
True or False	In South Carolina, a person must be eighteen years old to play a pinball machine.
True or False	Fish may not be contained in fishbowls while on a public bus in Oklahoma.

Permission granted by the authors of CORE Activities and Games for Technical Training to reproduce this page.

☐ ☐ ☐ # I HEARD THAT!

Author: Scott Enebo

Description: There are things we do in our work so often that they can start to lose significance. This can translate to sloppy customer service, unmotivated workers or, in general, subpar work. To help reenergize workers and get them thinking about the details of their work and the importance of each action, use "I Heard That!" to start a conversation about the current state and what can be done instead. This is based on two games called Mad Gab and Babble On.

Objective: Raise awareness of how repeated tasks can seem old, but action can be taken to help the purpose and meaning of the work come through.

Time: 5-10 minutes

Audience: Any training audience

Group Size: Any

Materials: I Heard That! phrases on PowerPoint slides

Process:

1. Get everyone into pairs and have one person seated facing the projection screen and one person seated facing away from the screen and looking at her partner.

2. Say, "In just a moment, I am going to show you a phrase on the screen. Each phrase phonetically sounds like a common phrase you may know, but the words look nothing like it. For example, you may see the words 'Elf Habits Hoop.' When read quickly, you will be able to hear the answer, which is 'Alphabet Soup.' The person facing the screen will be the reader, and the person facing away will try and guess the answer only by listening. You may find that you will need to read it more than once in order to have your partner guess correctly. Once you think you have the answer, stand up immediately. We will hear your guess and, if you are correct, you will get a point. The team with the most points at the end will win a semi-valuable prize!"

3. Begin showing phrases on the screen and hearing guesses.

4. Have partners switch halfway through so each can read and guess.

5. See which team had the most points and award a prize.

Note: Prizes can be as creative as you like. You can award a high-five from the trainer, a standing ovation from the class or even let the team with the most points help assign the length of the break.

Debrief:
1. What was it like doing this activity?
2. Which did you prefer: reading or guessing?
3. What tips did you find to make it easier to guess the correct answer?
4. Why is it hard to guess these even though they are relatively common phrases?
5. What correlation can you make between this activity and what we are going to discuss today?
6. Why is this something that we are going to spend time on today?
7. What is something that you do on a daily basis that can feel a bit like reading these phrases?
8. How do you imagine the people with whom you interact might interpret this?

Variations:
- Instead of putting the phrases up on a screen, make a set of cards with a phrase on one side and the answer on the back. This can become a table competition where a person will draw one of these cards and read it for the rest of the table. The person to the right of the reader will not guess but will know the correct answer. Once the phrase is guessed, the next person around the table will get a card. Continue for a set period of time and see which group gets the most correct answers.

- Use this activity as an energizer where you can intersperse these phrases throughout a session when you need a bit more energy in the room. Definitely encourage groups to stand when they have an answer to get the blood pumping.

http://bit.ly/CORETTIHT

Closers, Openers, Revisiters, Energizers

I Heard That! Phrases

Yore Luke Ink Hood	You're looking good
Up Hair Hush Ooze	A pair of shoes
Thick Awe Loved Hoot He	The call of duty
Space You'll Limp Picks	Special Olympics
Sex Yule Hair Is Mint	Sexual harassment
Loaf Meat Hender	Love Me Tender
Jog Clay Die Scream	Chocolate ice cream
Isle Of View	I love you
Hype People Earth Duh Hey	Happy birthday
Dew Ache Who Gulls Urge	Do a Google search
Eight He Muff Forces	A team of horses
Europe Art Tough Fit	You're a part of it
Mower Thin Nuke Inch Who	More than you can chew
Pea Sank White	Peace and quiet
Ah, Yah Dune Any Thin Turn Eight?	Are you doing anything tonight?
You Shore New Dull	Use your noodle
Dew Wino Hue	Do I know you?
Assess Seam Ease Heed	A sesame seed
Aid Hay Huff Ache Asian	A day of vacation
Ape Arrows Uncle As His	A pair of sunglasses
Bat Tree Snot Ink Looted	Batteries not included
Canoe Key Pass Egret	Can you keep a secret?
Delete Elmer Made	The little mermaid
Dish Hippie Slaw Stats He	The ship is lost at sea
Ice Mail Ask Hunk	I smell a skunk
Kitten Scene Gulf Aisle	Get in single file
Koala Deep Rod Ducks	Quality products
Mine Her Infer Auction	Minor infraction
Rim Him Birth Owl Limo	Remember the Alamo
Watch Choo Ear Nut Washer Tse	What you hear, not what you say
We Shy Worth Hare	Wish I were there
Weeg Lib His Neigh Sours	Weekly business hours
Will Saw Rim Ocean	Wheels are in motion
Dawned Hutch Debt Aisle	Don't touch that dial
Tote Hall Reek Hall	Total recall
Zola Reek Lips	Solar eclipse
Sell Your Laugh Hone	Cellular phone
Wreck You Lure Hoard He Calf	Regular or decaf?
Fur Stay Dins Trucked Her	First Aid instructor
Yang Keyed Ooh Dealt Andy	Yankee Doodle Dandy
Eight Hey Blanch Hair	A table and chair
Heart Official Ant Heller Gents	Artificial intelligence

Permission granted by the authors of CORE Activities and Games for Technical Training to reproduce this page.

KEYBOARD KINESTHETICS

Author: Rich Meiss

Description: Learners use a life-size keyboard to literally walk through a sequence.

Objective: To create an interactive way for participants to revisit content in a computer training program

Time: 10-20 minutes

Audience: Any technical training audience learning at computers

Group Size: Usually fewer than 15 people

Materials:
- One large bed sheet
- One box of markers

Process:
1. Get a large, light-colored bed sheet that you no longer need. Using dark markers, draw out a computer keyboard, marking large numbers, letters and symbols as represented on a real keyboard. Take the bed sheet to your class and lay it out in a large open area of the room.

2. After teaching a keying sequence on the computer, have the participants approach the sheet. Have them literally walk through the keying sequence they just learned making sure each participant takes a turn. When they are not taking their own turns, they can "coach" the other participants.

3. Continue this process throughout the training time, first teaching the content and then taking participants to the sheet to walk-through the process.

Debrief: A final walk-through can be done at the end of the program by going through all the steps.

Variations: Teach some of the concepts at the sheet and have a volunteer do the walk-through as you explain the process. Then ask the other participants to do their walk-through. This adds variety to the day and keeps the participants from settling into a standard pattern.

☐ ☐ ☐ LEARNING PASSPORT

Author: Marc Ratcliffe

Description: Like a travel passport, the learning passport collects information about the individual and identifies when they have reached certain learning destinations. This activity combines a number of different roles including an orienting tool, a get-to-know you activity, an energizer and a closing exercise.

Objective: To encourage self-reflection and interaction

Time: Throughout the day

Audience: Any

Group Size: Up to 20 people

Materials:
- Learning Passport templates
- Stampers
- Pens

Process:
1. Hand out the Learning Passports on the first day of training.
2. Ask participants to fill out their names and draw a head shot for themselves in the spaces provided. Next ask them to reflect on two problems or issues they hope this technical training will help solve. In effect, these will act as their goals for the program.
3. Once these are complete, issue every student a colored stamper and ask them to stamp their passports (on the correct page) as a reward for completing this task.
4. Explain that every time they work with someone new, they can get another stamp. The first person to fill his or her passport will be the winner and will receive a prize. (This could be a box of chocolates, a bottle of wine, a book or similar.)
5. Give participants their second stamp opportunity by asking them to move around to meet two or three other people to share two goals for the session.
6. Continue to provide passport stamp opportunities throughout the session.
7. At the end of the session, ask the participants to reflect on their two goals as part of a closing activity. People's sense of competition will drive them on in this quest. However, even those who are not normally competitive will tend to understand that the spirit of this activity is collaboration rather than competition.
8. To spice things up, provide "bonus stamp opportunities" where participants can get a stamp from you by doing something for you such as becoming a scribe, clearing the board, or collecting books.

Debrief: None

Variations: As a variation, the participants could come up with three or four specific goals for the session and only have their passports stamped once they complete their goals. Additionally, you could give the participants some additional goals to be met during the session and stamp their passports once these are fulfilled.

LEARNING PASSPORT

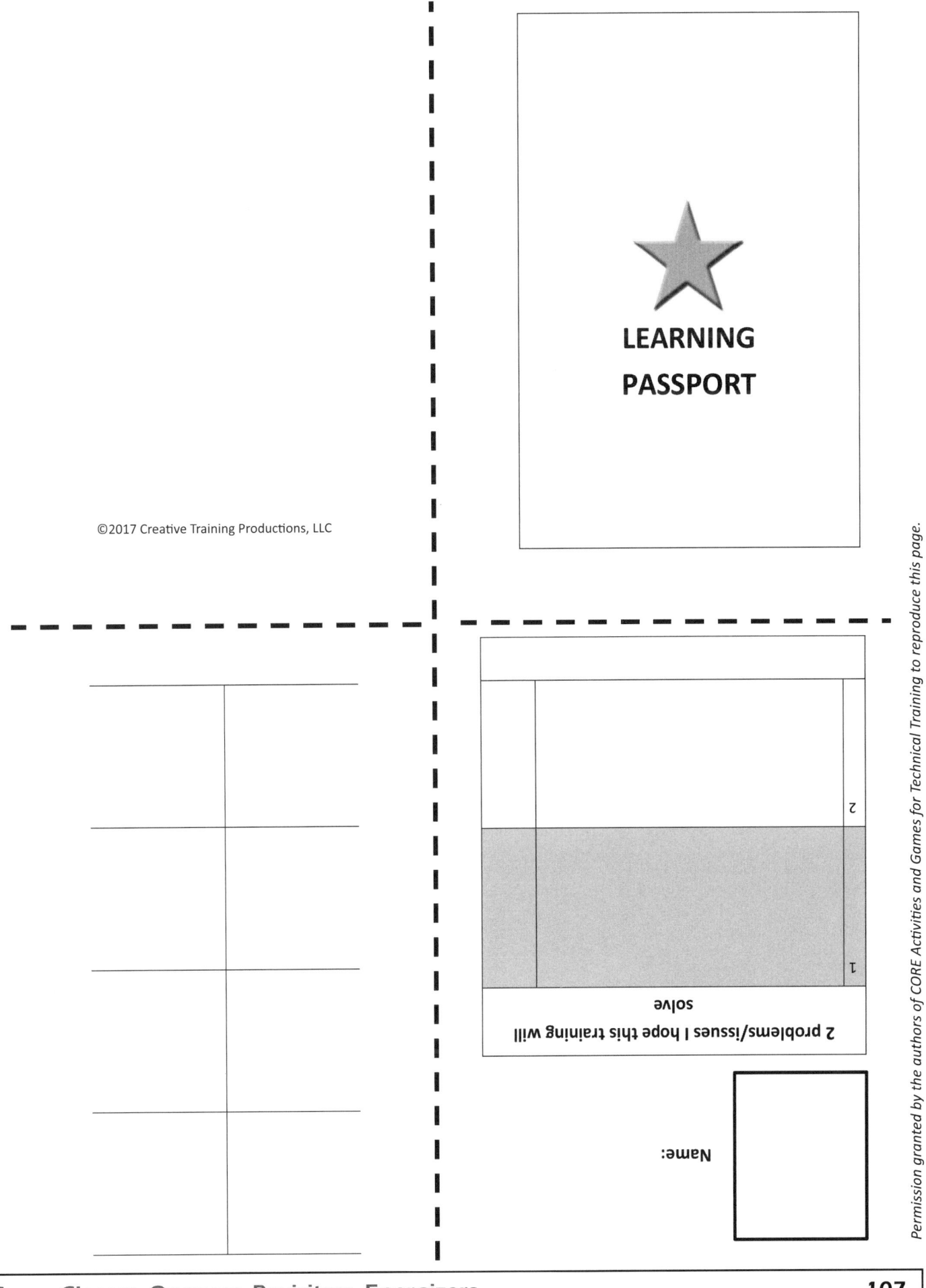

©2017 Creative Training Productions, LLC

2 problems/issues I hope this training will solve

Name:

Super Closers, Openers, Revisiters, Energizers

107

Permission granted by the authors of CORE Activities and Games for Technical Training to reproduce this page.

PROCESS STEPS POP UP

Author: Janice Horne

Description: Participants are assigned a step in the process and stand up when the trainer reads an action that belongs in their step.

Objective: To revisit key elements from a process

Time: 5 minutes

Audience: Any technical training audience

Group Size: 25 or fewer

Materials: Prepared information correlating to steps in the process (about 15 steps works best)

Process:
1. Determine how many major steps you have in your process. Group participants either by table or by counting off so that you have an equal number of participants representing each step. For example, if there are five steps in the process and there are five tables in the room, each table would be one step in the process.

2. Inform participants that you will be reading some key elements from the training that belong in certain steps in the process. When they hear something that belongs in the step their table represents, the whole table stands.

3. This is meant to go quickly to be an energizer and also cement learning.

Debrief: Ask if there's anything that the participants would like you to clarify from this activity.

Variations:
- Include a couple of items that fit in two or more of the steps in the process.
- For the last item you read, make it be something that would fit in each step of the process so that the whole room stands up at once.
- Use for regulatory or compliance training where each group represents a different regulation instead of a step in a process.
- Use this in sales training and insert steps in the selling process.

Super Closers, Openers, Revisiters, Energizers

REORGANIZATION ☐ ☐ ☐

Author: Marc Ratcliffe

Description: Reorganization is a regrouping exercise where participants have to quickly regroup based on different categories provided by the trainer. Some categories will be visually obvious, e.g. "group yourselves by hair color." Other categories will require additional discussion and negotiation, e.g. group yourselves by experience level.

Objective: To get people moving early and to reinforce the concept that some content is obvious and other content requires a deeper consideration.

Time: 10 minutes

Audience: Any training audience

Group Size: Any size

Materials: None

Process:
1. Explain to the participants that they have to form groups based on categories the trainer provides. Begin with a visual category such as eye color, hair color, or clothing type and have them form their first groups.

2. Next, regroup them by giving a new category. Below are some examples:
   - home location or geographic origin
   - birthday
   - work role
   - recreational pursuits

3. Continue the regrouping process until the participants have been sufficiently mixed up around the room.

Debrief: Discuss how they formulated groups and whether some categories were easier than others. Relate this to the content at hand by explaining that some learning/content/workplace tasks appear obvious while others require a deeper review and collaboration with others to get a full understanding.

Explore any variations in the categories by individual groups. For example, when grouping by birthday, some groups may connect based on birth month, others by birth year and some by season. Discuss the implications for the organization when people look at the same things in different ways.

Variations: As an extension, this activity could be used to determine learning preferences that can assist the trainer in customizing the training to the participants. For example, the trainer could ask the participants to regroup into those who would prefer reading a book, writing a letter or playing sudoku as a leisure activity. Based on their responses, you could gain some insight into their language, literacy and numeracy preferences.

Closers, Openers, Revisiters, Energizers

TECHNICAL ANAGRAMS

Author: Priscilla Shumway

Description: Participants look at an anagram and deduce what technical vocabulary word can be made from the anagram.

Objective: To get teams working together and networking while introducing or revisiting technical jargon

Time: 5 minutes

Audience: Any technical training audience

Group Size: Any

Materials: Flip chart or PowerPoint slide

Process: An anagram is a word or phrase formed by rearranging the letters of another word or phrase. Using this website [www.wordsmith.org/anagram], you can create anagrams from your vocabulary words by simply typing in the word.

1. Divide the group up into teams or pairs, depending on the size of the audience.
2. Give them 2 minutes to try and deduce the technical term from the anagram.

For example:

Vocabulary Term	Anagram
Technical	Cancel hit
Computer	Recto Ump
Nuclear	Can Rule
Software	Swear Oft
Application	Topical Pain

Debrief: How do these anagrams serve as a metaphor for a new learner to your content areas?

Variation: Allow the participants to create their own anagrams and use as a revisit or soft opener.

Closers, Openers, Revisiters, Energizers

TRAINING MUSICAL CHAIRS ☐ ☐ ☐

Author: Adrianne Roggenbuck

Description: Using the basis of Musical Chairs, participants will move around while the music is going and then sit down quickly in someone else's chair when the music stops. The learners will then read a blog post on today's training topic written on that computer.

Objective: To identify one to three key learnings from a segment of training and get energized by physically moving around the room to view each other's blog posts

Time: 5-8 minutes

Audience: Any technical training audience

Group Size: 5-15 people

Materials:
- Computers
- Upbeat music

Process:
1. Give participants 2 minutes to write a blog entry that describes what they have learned during the last segment of content.

2. Inform the group that they will be playing a form of Musical Chairs. They are to stand up and walk around the room while the music plays. When the music stops, they need to sit down in someone else's seat. They then have 30-60 seconds to read that person's entry before the music starts and the process repeats.

3. Each time the music stops, they must sit in a new seat. They may not sit in their own seats until the activity has concluded.

4. Stop the activity after a few rotations. Every person does not have to see each entry.

5. Have participants return to their original seats.

This activity may be repeated at different times during a multi-day training.

Debrief: Ask participants to share any new insights they gained from reading each other's blogs. Clarify any misconceptions and answer any questions they might have.

Variations:
- If participants do not have blogs, have them simply open a Word document to type their key learnings.
- The participants who view the entry may comment on it if you give them 1-2 minutes rather than 30 seconds.

Closers, Openers, Revisiters, Energizers

VIRTUAL TOUR ☐ ☐ ☐

Author: Becky Pike Pluth

Description: Energize your participants by taking them on a virtual tour of the system by "marching" across the keyboard or "surfing" the intranet.

Objective: Engage both the mind and the body in a physical "tour" of your technical content.

Time: 3-5 minutes

Audience: Any training audience

Group Size: Any size

Materials: Components of your technical training to insert into the virtual tour

Process:
1. Ask participants to stand up.
2. Lead the group on a virtual tour of the system or process. Participants should move for at least 10 seconds for each action. Below is an example, but you would want to insert your concepts.
   a. March across the keyboard.
   b. Surf the intranet for our website.
   c. Climb through the tabs to our portal.
   d. Stomp on the mouse for not working.
   e. Collect up all the pieces and throw them in the garbage.
   f. Crawl through the landing page to the data entry info.
   g. Hit ESC at anytime to exit the task.
   h. Pick the tab to enter customer info.
   i. Hit save; repeat.
   j. You are awesome for completing all the tasks! Now wave good bye to the document as you hit 'send.'

Additional movements to include may be: advance, break, crawl, creep, dart, dash, drive, escape, exit, flee, fly, go, hike, hurry, jog, kick, lead, leap, lumber, move, pass, progress, push, race, rush, skip, ski, slog, stir, stomp, tear, tour, trek, troop, walk, and whisk

Debrief: None

Variations: Have participants work in pairs to create their own virtual tour for a segment of the training and then lead the group through their journey. This then becomes a revisiter and an energizer.

http://bit.ly/CORETTVirtual

Closers, Openers, Revisiters, Energizers

ZIP ZAP ZOP

Author: Becky Pike Pluth contributor, original author unknown

Description: Many improvisation groups use this exercise as a warm-up before going on stage to establish trust, to encourage quick thinking and to loosen up a bit. I use this exercise, for a short period of time, to get the energy up in the room and to create laughter-reducing tension.

Objective: To break-up a longer section of content and reengage and re-focus a learner or group

Time: 5-10 minutes

Audience: Any

Group Size: 6 or more people

Materials: None

Process:
1. Have the entire group form a circle in your classroom. If in a computer-based classroom, have learners move to a part of the wall closest to their row.

2. One person will quickly clap and point at another person in the circle while saying "zip." The person who received the "zip" becomes the "zapper." This person will quickly clap and point to another in the circle while saying "zap." The person who received the "zap" now becomes the "zopper." This person will quickly clap and point at another in the circle, while saying "zop." The person who received the "zop" becomes the "zipper" and the cycle begins again, "zip, zap, zop, zip, zap, zop…"

3. The goal is to pass the "zip, zap, zop" around the room as quickly as possible to increase the energy. This is harder than it may appear, which is why the room fills with laughter quite quickly.

Debrief: None

Variations: If you are training in a regular room (not a computer room), have the group members form a circle by placing their own palms together in front of them. In this scenario, the word "zip" means left, "zap" means right and "zop" is across the circle. Whomever begins the game chooses the word to begin with. With her palms together in front of her, the first volunteer says the word and points in the proper direction. The zip, zap or zop continues that direction until someone uses a different word. For example, if I start with "zip," my hands would send the "zip" to my left. The next person would do the same and say "zip," and it would continue until someone says something different such as "zop," and now it heads across the circle. When people make a mistake, they can sit out or the cycle can begin again.

http://bit.ly/CORETTZZZZ

Closers, Openers, Revisiters, Energizers

YOUR NAME IN LIGHTS!

Your name can SHOW UP IN LIGHTS as a contributor of a closer, an opener, a revisiter or an energizer in our next publication.

Design and create any sort of opening and closing exercises.

Find new and creative ways to energize your participants and review or summarize content.

If we publish your idea in our next CORE book, you'll receive an updated copy with "YOUR NAME IN LIGHTS!"
Copy this page and use the copy for your submission. Describe/draw your idea briefly but completely.
Use the lines below and another sheet if necessary. Or send your submission by e-mail to rmeiss@bobpikegroup.com.
We'll give you full credit for any ideas published.

_____

_____

_____

_____

_____

_____

_____

YOUR NAME: _____

COMPANY (IF APPLICABLE): _____

ADDRESS: _____

PHONE: _____ FAX: _____

E-MAIL: _____

Submit ideas to:

The Bob Pike Group

14530 Martin Drive

Eden Prairie, MN 55344

Fax: 952-829-0260

www.bobpikegroup.com

Closers, Openers, Revisiters, Energizers

ABOUT THE AUTHORS

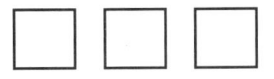

Becky Pike Pluth, M.Ed., CSP, MPCT
With more than 20 years as a training professional and two training industry best-selling books on the market, Becky Pike Pluth, The Bob Pike Group's president and CEO, doesn't rest on her laurels. As proof of her desire to continuously strive for "great," Becky was named one of *Training* magazine's Top 40 under 40 in 2012. She is the author of *Creative Training* and *Webinars with WoW Factor* along with several other books.

Rich Meiss, MBA, MPCT
Rich has been a participant-centered trainer with Bob Pike and other leading train-the-trainer organizations for more than 25 years. He has designed and taught numerous workshops to more than 65,000 trainers and leaders worldwide. His personal approach causes audiences to warm to him instantly. Most of his work is with repeat clients who continue to ask specifically for him. Rich is author or co-author of 10 books including *Coaching for Results* and *CORE: Activities and Games for Face-to-Face Training, volume 3*.

Karen Carlson, MPCT
With more than 15 years of experience in learning and development, Karen has a proven track record of exceeding customer expectations and catering delivery and materials to the unique needs of each client. She includes adult learning methodology and recognizes the diverse learning styles of her audiences when designing materials.

Scott Enebo, M.A., MPCT
Scott Enebo is a strong advocate and model for creative and interactive training as he continues to see the impact it has on the participants experiencing the learning. Scott received his master's degree in intercultural relations with a focus on multicultural training. He also is trained in the ICA's Technology of Participation and enjoys conducting participatory strategic planning and action planning sessions.

Janice Horne, MPCT
Janice has a drive and enthusiasm for training and is motivated by the end result—an improved training experience by those who learn from her participants. Having thrived in retail, financial, and government organizations, Janice brings a wealth of skills to adult learning to help businesses focus on results-based action. Janice also is author of *The ABCs for Happy Living*.

Marc Ratcliffe, M.Ed., MPCT
Marc founded MRWED Training and Assessment in Brisbane, Australia in 2000 which quickly became one of Australia's leading providers of trainer training. It has received numerous awards including the 2010 LearnX award for Best Workplace Trainer Training Program. Marc was recently named Queensland/Northern Territory Learning and Development Person of the Year for 2013 by the Australia Institute of Learning and Development. He is the author of The *Trainer's Toolkit* and *The Trainer's Cook Book*.

Adrianne Roggenbuck, M.Ed., MPCT

Since joining The Bob Pike Group, Adrianne has championed Research-based Creative Teaching Strategies and Designing Lessons that SCORE, two workshops specifically for teachers. As a dynamic, memorable and inspirational trainer, Adrianne presents regularly at education conferences. She also is an adjunct instructor for graduate-level classes at Aurora University and Waubonsee Community College in Aurora, Ill.

Priscilla Shumway, M.Ed., MPCT

As a senior trainer for The Bob Pike Group, Priscilla brings a wealth of experience in adult education and technical training to her sessions and is a two-time recipient of the Pike's Peak Performer Award for content and facilitator performance. Priscilla has advanced studies in Accelerated Learning, Integrative Learning and Learning Styles. She also was a contributing author to *The Experts' Guide to the K-12 School Market*.

OTHER BOOKS BY THESE AUTHORS

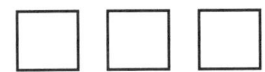

101 Movie Clips that Teach and Train

Using short clips from movies can relay learning points more dramatically and quickly than any lecture.

Let this award-winning book jumpstart your creativity for lesson planning or training design by providing you with the perfect movie clip for over 100 topics including discrimination, leadership, team building, and sales.

Each clip comes with cueing times, plot summary and scene context, and cogent discussion questions. All topics are cross-referenced so you can easily find the perfect clip for your teaching or training needs.

CORE Series

The CORE! series is a compilation of activities that will help engage your learners while ensuring your content is remembered long after class is over.

These activities for **Closing** your session with impact, **Opening** your session with relevance, **Revisiting** content creatively, and **Energizing** your learners will make you a learning legend and improve training retention.

Books in this series include general CORE activities as well as a focus on technical, webinar, and one-on-one training.

Books in this series include:

Activities and Games for Face-to-Face Training, volume 3

Activities and Games for Webinars, volume 5

Activities and Games for One-on-One Training, volume 6

Webinars with WoW Factor

Death by webinar is rapidly replacing death by PowerPoint!

Make webinars effective and engaging.

Teaching online is a different animal—requiring different skills and a different energy—that completely exposes any weaknesses in your material and preparation. In this book, Becky Pike Pluth shows trainers where to start when moving to an online platform and what pitfalls to avoid along with explaining basic webinar tools trainers can use to make online training interactive. Becky includes 40 activities that will help even a novice webinar trainer create an online training that has impact and builds in long-term retention.

Creative Training

Cut your design time in half, increase learner retention, and have more fun! It's the trainer's trifecta, and it can be achieved through Instructor-Led, Participant-Centered (ILPC) creative training.

In this book, Becky Pike Pluth, CEO of The Bob Pike Group, the pioneer in Creative Training Techniques®, explains why creative training works and walks the reader through a step-by-step process so you can implement these methods, experience improved training results, and reignite your passion for training.

All these titles and more great resources for training effectively are available from The Bob Pike Group at www.BobPikeGroup.com/product or by calling (952) 829-2658 or (800) 383-9210.